APPRENTICES OUT OF THEIR TIME

SOCIETY TODAY AND TOMORROW

General Editor: A. H. Halsey

Apprentices Out of Their Time

A FOLLOW-UP STUDY

ETHEL VENABLES

The word 'apprentice' is used to denote young workers whose conditions of employment allowed them to attend a local technical college for academic study for at least one day per week. Most of them were paid an 'apprentice' or junior wage which was less than that paid to comparable workers aged twenty-one and over. Thus, whether indentured or not, most of them 'served their time' for five years from sixteen to twenty-one before qualifying for adult status.

FABER AND FABER
3 Queen Square London

First published in 1974
by Faber and Faber Limited
3 Queen Square London WC1
Printed in Great Britain by
Western Printing Services Limited Bristol

ISBN 0 571 10524 6

© *1974* by Ethel Venables

Contents

Preface

The follow-up study reported in this book is concerned with 2,000 young men aged over twenty-one in 1966. All had participated in previous studies when they were first-year students in day-release classes at various local technical colleges. It is important to note the nature of the sample: as school leavers they were all 'unqualified' i.e. they had not obtained the necessary standard of 'O' level success to entitle them to direct entry into an Ordinary National Certificate class and indeed most of them had not attempted 'O' level examinations at all. About 60 per cent were ex-secondary modern school pupils, most of the rest being divided almost equally between technical and grammar schools. Approximately 5 per cent had attended 'other' schools i.e. comprehensive, special and private schools.

At least 90 per cent were engineering apprentices and most of those from selective schools were taking National Certificate courses. The rest were divided between a variety of craft courses, some electrical and some mechanical. The additional 10 per cent were students of either building, catering or commerce.

The first two studies were carried out in four colleges in Manchester in 1950 and 1952 and the third, which dealt with a sample of O.N.C. students only, was done in three local colleges in Birmingham beginning in 1957. These results were published in the professional journals.[1]

The last and most comprehensive study started in 1960 in one Birmingham college and was financed by the Nuffield Foundation. The report was published under the title *The Young Worker at College – a Study of a Local Tech*. (Faber and Faber) in January 1967. By this time even the youngest members of the latest sample were 'out of their time'. Those few who were only fifteen when the

[1] See Bibliography, Appendix I.

9

1960 study began reached twenty-one in 1966 and the oldest subjects, from the 1950 study, were at least thirty-one. Several of them were in their late thirties.

The data available on all these people was very varied, since the four projects had all been carried out with different purposes in mind. The first was an investigation of the reserve of ability in technical colleges, the second a selection and placement study, the third was concerned with the discrepancy between verbal and non-verbal ability among such students and the improvement in verbal ability during the years at college, and the fourth was a study of one institution. However, there was sufficient overlap to make a combined follow-up study feasible. Two of the tests used were common to all and data on age, social class, schooling and size of employing firm had been recorded in most cases. Examination results during the first three years were also known.

The justification of a follow-up in any system is the provision of relevant information about outcomes which can be fed back into the system in order to improve performance. The paucity of information is understandable in view of the in-out nature of the part-time day-release system and the pressure on technical college staff. The potential pay-off from the monitoring of human resources is not yet generally appreciated.

The study was made possible by the continued generosity of the Nuffield Foundation who provided finance for myself and a secretary for a further three years. During the first two, we remained in the Education Department of the University of Birmingham and the final year was spent at the University of Aston in Birmingham alongside the team of research workers there (directed by Mr. Derek Pugh – now Professor Pugh), who were making an empirical study of work organisation.

I am sincerely grateful to Professor Peel of Birmingham for allowing me to continue to work in his department; to Mr. Pugh and his colleagues and the administrative staff of the University of Aston for making me welcome and, most particularly, to the Trustees of the Nuffield Foundation, the then Director, Mr. Brian Young, and Dr. Kenneth Blyth.

I have to thank Mr. D. J. Rees of Edinburgh for making one of his programmes available to me. Mr. Bowcock, Director, and Mrs. Parker, formerly Senior Programmer, of the Computer Centre at Aston modified it to suit the requirements of this study, and piloted the resultant tapes through the Atlas Computer of the University of London. I am greatly indebted to them for the large amount of work which has been done in their department.

The National Survey under the direction of Dr. J. W. B. Douglas is now in its twenty-eighth year. The longitudinal study of secondary education *All Our Future* was published in 1968 and the next stage dealing with school leavers at work and college is awaited with great interest. I am indebted to Dr. Douglas and two of the members of his staff who have been concerned with the school leavers survey – David Nelson in the early stages and now Nicola Cherry – for their kindness in keeping me informed about its progress.

I have had stalwart secretarial assistance from four people. Mrs. Pat Mallatratt who was my assistant on the study of *The Young Worker at College* saw this project through with her usual cheerfulness and efficiency up to the preparation of the data tape. With the analysis of the print-outs I had some valuable part-time help from Miss Mary Page and Mrs. Gillian Ellis. Latterly, and particularly over the typing and retyping of the manuscript and its tables, I have been fortunate in having the expert assistance of Mrs. Jo Dixon.

Since my retirement from a full-time appointment with the University of Aston in Birmingham, I have continued to work here in an honorary capacity. For the provision of accommodation and the use of the library and other resources I am greatly indebted to the University and to the Vice-Chancellor, Dr. J. A. Pope.

I am indebted to a number of people with whom I have discussed the present state and future prospects of the local colleges including some Principals of local colleges and Education Officers who must remain anonymous. I would like to express my thanks particularly to Mr. A. D. Collop, H.M.C.I.; Sir Cyril English, Director-General, City and Guilds of London Institute; Mr. F. Metcalfe, C.B.E., Director, Engineering Industry Training Board; Mr. E. W. Sudale, H.M.S.I.; and Dr. J. T. Young, Principal, Warley College of Technology. The author is solely responsible for the views expressed.

Those who maintain that two academics in one household is at least one too many, do not realise the enormous advantage of having one's most candid critic readily available. So to my husband, Sir Peter Venables, without whom . . ., I say simply thank you.

ETHEL VENABLES
University of Aston in Birmingham
1973

CHAPTER 1

Background to the Research

In the course of the four studies listed in the Preface a large body of data was accumulated about 'unqualified' school leavers who had taken on an engineering apprenticeship and about their chances of success in the technical college examinations. Of the O.N.C. students in the first two samples only 9 or 10 per cent succeeded in obtaining a certificate in the minimum period of three years. The study commissioned by the Crowther Committee[1] gave an estimated maximum figure for the success rate in even time (i.e. three years) of 11 per cent. Some attempt was made to improve both placement and treatment in my 1960 study and the percentage of starters in possession of an Ordinary National Certificate at the end of three years was 19.[2]

The correlations between examination success and measures of intelligence were – as expected – positive but small, i.e. many failing students had high scores. The small groups of students who registered for a course but did not take the first-year examination (drop-outs) had in most cases higher mean scores than the failing students and on some tests, such as for example a vocabulary test, higher mean scores than the successful ones.

Follow-up studies of students both here and in the States have shown that many 'drop-outs' are able persons who are dissatisfied with the education provided. The number of such 'misfits' has been shown to be large enough to warrant both better facilities for educational and vocational guidance and re-examination of the teaching–learning process.

With part-time technical college students there is the further complication that they are attempting to do two things at once. They are each learning to do a job which differs from firm to firm and studying for examinations which at best they see as only partially

[1] *15 to 18*, H.M.S.O., 1959.
[2] Venables, E., *The Young Worker at College*, p. 142.

13

related to their practical work and at worst totally irrelevant. The keen student may see the College work as an investment in the future but personality factors and family background affect a person's ability to take the long-term view. The attitudes of the employer and the firm's policy towards trainees are an important influence on the student's motivation and in all the four initial researches the success rates for apprentices in the larger firms (1,000 employees or more) were higher than for the rest and this result was unrelated to the level of measured intelligence. In these samples of 'unqualified' recruits those taken on by the large firms were on the whole less able in terms of test scores than those employed by the smaller firms. The large firms recruit at all levels of ability and presumably therefore absorb also a high proportion of the qualified leavers who enter industry direct from school.

There are two possible reasons for the superior achievement of 'large firm' apprentices. The existence of an 'educational department' plus a policy and an assigned officer to go with it demonstrates to the recruit that academic attainment is recorded and valued; secondly he is more likely to be one of a group of beginners studying together which provides a more stimulating educational atmosphere than that enjoyed by the lone apprentice in a smaller firm.

In the earlier studies on which this present one is based records of the success and failure of the student-workers were kept for three years and in the case of the 1950 study were extended to five. Most of them, as is usual with apprentices, stayed with the same firm during those years. The old indentured apprentice used to 'serve his time' for seven years and this was gradually reduced to five. Wage agreements are (or have been) largely based on the assumption of a five-year learnership. At twenty-one the 'boy' who was 'taken on' at sixteen is 'out of his time', and becomes a 'journeyman' – an adult worker entitled to a day's pay for a day's work. This often meant, though not always, that he left the master under whom he had been trained and the tendency to leave the place where you are remembered as 'Young Tom the apprentice' still persists.

Once the fourth of my series of studies was completed, and all the 2,000 or so subjects had had time to become adult workers, it was decided to try to discover what 'serving their time' had meant to them and where their 'journeyings' had led them. This involved devising a questionnaire to be sent to all those who could be traced and in addition it was decided to try to interview a random sample.

The problems of manpower utilisation are an increasing concern alike of government, industrial managers and the trade unions and there is an undoubted need for studies of the relationship between education and occupation. The Unit for Economic and Statistical Studies at L.S.E. under the direction of Professor Claus Moser published a preliminary report on 'The Utilisation of Educated Manpower in Industry' in 1967.[1] The authors' final conclusion in this pilot study was 'that sophisticated manpower planning involving either detailed occupational and educational projections or, more ambitious still, estimates of an optimal occupational and educational structure is out of the question at this time.

'Few firms, without a great deal of effort, would be able unaided to provide an accurate picture of their occupational structure at a point of time, or its changes over time; even fewer would be able to provide details of the educational structure of their labour force.'

Secondly they suggest that 'it is worth while paying more attention to the degree of flexibility of educational requirements for particular occupations. Although we have not been able to ascertain optimal educational requirements, we have been able to establish both that the same occupation is staffed by people of varying educational backgrounds and experience, and also that it is not the case that one particular education-experience requirement stands out as obviously appropriate for each occupation.'[2]

The authors are economists and were concerned to study the rate of return in investment in education and their preliminary findings suggest that the return is much higher at 'the middle pre-degree' level than at degree level itself, confirming the view that there is a shortage of highly qualified technicians.

Denis Pym[3] in a paper dealing with the 'misuse' of professional manpower rejected the idea that Britain is short of manpower and complained that research on manpower problems had only been marginally concerned with utilisation citing by way of illustration the two Command Papers 3102 and 3103.[4] Pym considers that 'some of our economic difficulties stem from our failure to recognise

[1] By Blaug M., Preston M. H. and Ziderman A. Oliver Boyd.
[2] Ibid., pp. 82–3.
[3] Pym, Denis, 'Technical Change and the Misuse of Professional Manpower: Some Studies and Observations', *Occupational Psychology*, Vol. 41, January 1967, pp. 1–16.
[4] Committee on Manpower Resources for Science and Technology. Cmnd. 3102, H.M.S.O., 1966. *Report on the 1965 Triennial Manpower Survey of Engineers, Technologists, Scientists and Technical Supporting Staff.* Cmnd. 3103, H.M.S.O., 1966. *Interim Report of the Working Group on Manpower Parameters for Scientific Growth.*

and accept the decline in the "gospel of work".' Even among employees in progressive firms he claims to have found 'a widespread disinclination to regard industriousness as a moral virtue'. In his research he has been primarily interested in 'underemployment' rather than 'misemployment' of skill and in a series of studies has monitored the dissatisfaction of qualified scientists and technologists with the conditions of their industrial employment.

Other writers attempt to conceptualise the interaction between individuals and organisations. In a work on 'Organisational Stress' Robert Kahn[1] and his associates underline the importance of the idea of role as a unifying concept and in an excellent summary of the contribution of the Behavioural Sciences to organisational studies Warren Bennis[2] in his concluding paragraph writes:

The remarkable aspect of our generation is its commitment to change, in thought and action. Our educational system should (1) help us to identify with this adaptive process without fear of losing our identity, (2) increase our tolerance of ambiguity without the fear of losing intellectual mastery, (3) increase our ability to collaborate without fear of losing individuality, (4) develop a willingness to participate in social evolution while recognising implacable forces. In short we need an educational system which can help us to make a virtue out of contingency rather than one which induces hesitancy and its reckless companion, expedience.

Two more recent studies by economists have investigated the economic return on investment in tertiary education.[3] Vera Morris and Adrian Ziderman (1971)[4] argue that because of increasing costs 'the scale and scope of higher education provision should be carefully planned to achieve appropriate balances between it and other demands on public expenditure. . . .' Their article presents 'some first results of the cost-benefit study of higher education expenditure undertaken by the Planning Branch of the Department of Education and Science' which show 'as the most realistic view of rates of

[1] Kahn R., Wolfe D., Quinn R., Snock J. D. and Rosenthal R., *Organisational Stress*, John Wiley & Sons Inc., N.Y., 1964.

[2] Bennis, Warren G., *Changing Organisations*, McGraw-Hill, 1966, pp. 180–209.

[3] Some of the material at the end of this Chapter and on pp. 121–126 in Chapter 7 was published in *Higher Education*, Vol. 1, No. 3, August 1972. Permission to quote is gratefully acknowledged.

[4] 'The Economic Return on Investment in Higher Education in England and Wales,' *Economic Trends*, No. 211, pp. xx–xxxi.

return to society' an incremental rate of over 20 per cent for a Higher National Certificate through 12·4 per cent for a first degree down to 2·7 per cent for a doctorate.

This study was heavily criticised by other economists on various grounds including, for example, the impossibility of putting a price on the 'benefits' of education (John Vaizey, 1971)[1] and, in the case of part-time H.N.C. students, relating their success in terms of salary to the actual possession of the certificate rather than to the qualities of persistence and drive needed to stay the course (Ernest Rudd, 1971).[2] Willem van der Eyken (*Further Education*, 1971)[3] has criticised not so much the research itself but the interpretation of the results. Instead of concluding that graduate studies should be cut back we should be asking the question 'why it is that in British industry these rather poor rates of return should prevail'. Since rates of pay for technicians range very widely it is 'to some extent misleading to average out payments of this kind . . . as this smooths out the very differences that matter in this argument'. It is also 'not wildly improbable that many graduates are underemployed and consequently underpaid by industry'.

The two writers under attack are of course aware that rates of return to *society* do not include any allowance for what they call 'positive consumption and externality effects' and recognise that some of their procedures 'are extremely crude'. Indeed their paper concludes with the statement that 'these purely economic aspects of education are not necessarily the most important', but nevertheless concern about the conclusions which might be drawn from such studies by those in charge of the allocation of resources is inevitable.

In the study of 'Qualified Manpower and Economic Performance' (Layard et al., 1971)[4] similar findings about the low cost of part-time education for H.N.C. are reported and the authors conclude that 'there is no clear case for deliberately discouraging it in favour of the more costly full-time courses.' They concede that private costs such as the cost of foregone leisure (which is particularly high for those who have to attend evening classes) are not included in the calculations but they insist that the figures reached by this type of economic analysis do convey 'a real point: part-time education may

[1] Vaizey, J., 'Ask a Silly Question', *The Times Educational Supplement*, 2.7.71, p. 4.

[2] Rudd, E., 'Sample of Error', *The Times Educational Supplement*, 2.7.71, p. 4.

[3] Editorial, *Further Education*, Summer 1971, p. 119.

[4] Layard, P. R. G., Sargan J. D., Ager M. E. and Jones D. J., *Qualified Manpower and Economic Performance*, Allen Lane, 1971.

be poor quality and its products may not command high salaries but it is very cheap. Those who argue for ever higher quality need to consider the case for "more, worse and cheaper".' Clearly the point the economists make *is* 'real' but it is not the only 'real point' to be made and the case *against* 'more, worse and cheaper' also needs consideration.

The results of this study provide some evidence of the human and social costs of part-time further education and of the feelings engendered among those who were offered an educational experience which is now being openly admitted to be worse than and cheaper than that which was offered to their more privileged contemporaries.

CHAPTER 2

The First Stage

There were three main tasks in setting up this enquiry: the first was to devise a questionnaire, a copy of which is reprinted as Appendix IV. It provided for eighty items of information (each allowed a scale of up to ten points) divided into six sections. Section I asked for biographical details: date of birth, age on leaving school, type of school attended, school examinations passed, number of siblings and father's job. The results of this section are recorded in Chapter 3. Section II dealt with industrial experience and training including the type of firm at which the learner served his time (Chapter 4). Section III related to technical college achievement (Chapter 5) and the relevance of the academic study to the subsequent employment (Chapter 6). Section IV asked for assessments of satisfaction and the improvements respondents would like to see for the next generation of students (Chapter 7). Section V had only one question – willingness to be interviewed.

Some of the eighty items were reserved for test results which were culled from the original record cards: six additional derived items were added making eighty-six in all. For example items 2 and 3 listed all the courses (nineteen in all) represented in the total sample. From these an additional item on a three-point scale was derived dividing the courses into O.N.C. Mechanical Trades and Electrical Trades. Again the recording of the family structure required four items with a possible forty 'bits'. This was reduced to one item with ten bits which made it possible to calculate, for example, the number of only children, first-borns, younger sons, etc.

The parts of Mr. Rees's programme which were used in the analysis of the results were: one-way and two-way contingency tables; Chi square tests and Kendall's Tau test on all two-way tables; means and standard deviations on all test scores.

The second task was to find the subjects. Record cards giving (among other items) name, date of birth and the name (i.e. area) of their first college were available for 2,254 persons. For those concerned in the two Birmingham studies in 1957 and 1960 addresses had either been recorded, or were still available in the colleges. This meant that for this group reminders could be sent to those not responding within ten days or so. To contact the Manchester subjects we relied on the help of the Ministry of Pensions and National Insurance who were able to direct 83 per cent of the envelopes that we sent to them.[1]

Tables 2.1 and 2.2 set out the overall response and indicate the figures on which the subsequent analysis of engineering students was based.

Several parents replied on behalf of their sons mostly to say that they were now married and that the form was being redirected. Some were unhappy letters calling for a personal reply. It is a hazard of postal enquiries that not all the subjects can be expected to be alive,

TABLE 2.1

Total Response

	Manchester samples 1950 and 1952	Birmingham samples 1957 and 1960	Totals
Number of cards available	1067	1187	2254
Addresses recorded	nil	1187	
Returned by G.P.O.	—	67	
Traced by M.P.N.I.	889	34 (out of 67)	
Returned by G.P.O.	7	—	
Total assumed delivered	882 (83%)	1154 (97%)	2036 (90%)
Number of respondents	222	492[2]	714
Proportion	25%	43%	36%

[1] I would like to record my gratitude here and to say how helpfully and expeditiously this was done. No breach of confidence was involved as no addresses were disclosed. An explanatory letter was enclosed with the questionnaire and we were only able to correspond with those subjects who returned the form and included an address on it.

[2] This figure includes some subjects who needed a reminder before responding but this factor alone does not account for the much larger response rate of the Birmingham students.

well and happy. Some sons were said to have 'gone away'. 'You had better forget it,' wrote one unhappy mother: her son had gone away and wouldn't be back (out?) for some time. Two recorded a death, another serious disability, another a motor accident and so on. Several individuals wrote to say that they had 'changed from engineering' so the form 'didn't apply' to them. Some, but only some, were persuaded by our subsequent explanations to reply.

TABLE 2.2

Engineering students and 'others'

	Respondents	Remainder 'at risk'[1]	Total 'at risk'
Totals	714	1540	2254
Engineering students only	646[2]	1505	2151
Other students[3]	68	35	103

Once the replies were received, the third task, before undertaking the full analysis of the answers, was to draw a random sample representative not of the respondents only, but of the total sample 'at risk'. To draw this it was necessary to establish the bias of the respondents in relation to the information available on the total set of records. Preliminary explorations of the small proportion of students who had had no failures in their first three years of college study suggested a possible source of bias. A complete analysis was therefore made (without benefit of a computer at this stage) of the response rates of these students assumed to have received a questionnaire, according to their success and failure as recorded on the cards. The bias in favour of those who were initially successful was found to be considerable. Response rates ranged from 60 per cent for the youngest members of the most successful group to 13 per cent for the older subjects who had absented themselves in the first year of their college studies.

[1] Because of the uncertainty about which of the non-respondents had in fact received a questionnaire it was decided to base any comparative analysis of the engineering students on all the record cards available.

[2] The 646 cards of the engineering respondents used for the computer analysis of the four separate samples were reduced (by accident) to 644 when 'total' sample was analysed.

[3] 'Other' students comprise all those not in engineering courses such as a few builders in the 1950 sample and students in the departments of commerce and catering in the 1960 study. This was a study of one college and all first-year students in that year were recorded. The apparently high response rate for this group is anomalous as many of their record cards were incomplete and these were excluded from the analysis of the non-respondents.

The decision was then taken to stratify the selection of the random sample on the basis of these figures in the hope of providing a sample more representative of those 'at risk' and offsetting as far as possible the bias in favour of examination success in the total sample of respondents. Table 2.3 gives detailed response rates and sets out the plan for the stratified random sample comprising 5 per cent of the older students and 10 per cent of the more recent ones. It was fortunate that there was enough response from the students who were initially the less successful to make this scheme possible. Among the absentees, for example, 8 out of 20 and 15 out of 27 had to be drawn. For those succeeding in their first year the proportions drawn for the interview samples were 17 out of 103 respondents and 44 out of 208 respectively.

160 cards were at first drawn (using random numbers) giving an interview sample representing about one in thirteen of the total numbers of 2,151 engineering students 'at risk' (7·4 per cent) and comprising approximately a quarter of the 646 engineering respondents. This was felt to be a manageable number to interview in the time available. Six others were drawn subsequently partly as a safeguard against refusals and also to ensure the inclusion of at least three or four of those who had transferred to block-release courses. Thus where there are differences in results between the total respondent sample and the interviewees in the tables throughout the book, the latter can be taken to be more representative of the total intake to the colleges. However, later analysis of the apparently less successful respondents revealed that a high proportion of them had in fact gone on to achieve success at a later stage (see p. 74) so that the interview sample is inevitably less representative of the starters than we had hoped.

Not every card which turned up in the draw could be accepted as only 82 per cent of the respondents had signified their willingness to be interviewed (item 80, p. 10 of the questionnaire). One form redirected by a parent, duly returned from Australia, indicating that an interview would be welcome, turned up in the randomising. Unhappily it had to be discarded! One person in 160 (0·6 per cent) represents thirteen in 2,151. Presumably there are more British-trained technicians in the far-flung Commonwealth than that, but the rest of the interview sample proved to be remarkably parochial. Nearly all were to be found within a radius of thirty miles of their original work places, many of them with the same firms. The likelihood of a response may well be inversely proportional to the distance

TABLE 2.3

Plan for the stratified selection of the random (interview) sample in relation to year of entry and to early success in college studies

		1950 and 1952 samples		1957 and 1960 samples		Totals		% in each of 4 categories
		N	Proportion	N	Proportion	N	Proportion	
1. Maximum success in first three years	Sample at risk	63	100%	208	100%	271	100%	13
	Respondents	29	45%	124	60%	153	56%	21
	Interview sample	4	6%	21	10%	25	9%	16
2. Passed first-year examination	Sample at risk	339	100%	439	100%	778	100%	38
	Respondents	103	30%	208	47%	311	40%	44
	Interview sample	17	5%	44	10%	61	7·8%	38
3. Failed first-year examination	Sample at risk	325	100%	355	100%	680	100%	34
	Respondents	70	22%	133	38%	203	30%	28
	Interview sample	16	5%	35	10%	51	7·5%	32
4. Absent first-year examination	Sample at risk	155	100%	152	100%	307	100%	15
	Respondents	20	13%	27	18%	47	15%	7
	Interview sample	8	5%	15	10%	23	7·5%	14
Totals	Sample at risk	882	100%	1154	100%	2036	100%	100
	Respondents	222	25%	492	43%	714	35%	100
	Interview sample	45	5%	115	10%	160	7·8%	100

moved from home so that there are no useful conclusions to be drawn here.

Timetabling the interviewing was an elaborate and time-consuming business, but once fixed, no appointment was broken. The choice of meeting place was theirs. A few offered to come to my office; one of these was working on the University site and the others were mainly salesmen for whom one more visit was all in the day's work. Of the rest about half took place in their homes during the evenings and the other half in a room, set aside for us, at the place of work. Each of the young men gave me at least an hour and those talks taking place at home in the evenings were often prolonged to include refreshments and a meeting with wife and family. For those couples tied to the home because of young children, a visit of this kind was clearly welcome for social reasons and I was told on several occasions that I was a 'change from the telly'. Among this group the main motivation in their willingness to be interviewed seemed to be a genuine interest in the problems of education, particularly in relation to their own children, and a concern about their own future and the general employment situation. Some of the less successful ones presented a very different picture and their responses could in some cases be seen as a cry for help.

The interviews were conducted as free-ranging discussions since the completed questionnaires had supplied all the hard facts needed and it was hoped to get the feel of their situation by allowing them to talk. However, two explicit topics were introduced into each discussion: how had the change from school to work been made and secondly, what ideas had they about the education of their own children, many of whom I met. The youngest was a week old and the oldest about ten years.

This book is about these 600 or so engineers who responded, often in a very personal way, to my request for information. A high proportion were willing to see me and I was actually able to visit a quarter of them. In many cases it was the second time I had interviewed them and, among the youngest ones, the previous study was clearly remembered. I feel very privileged to have been able to get to know these young men. I have already thanked them and their employers who allowed me to visit their firms, but I would like to express my gratitude publicly.

The main results of the survey are presented in the following five chapters. Some information obtained on the questionnaire had already been collated for one or other of the samples in the earlier

24

studies and only the briefest account will be given here of topics already dealt with in *The Young Worker at College*. The survey has enabled us to fill in some gaps in the information already recorded and to confirm some of the conclusions with a wider sample of students.

In relation to items entered on record cards, and therefore available for non-respondents, it was possible to calculate response rates but this has only been done where the records were reasonably complete, as they were, for example, on previous schooling, father's job, size of recruiting firm and initial course registration at the college.

The respondents can be grouped in various ways. The total group can be divided into two sub-groups according to initial course of study i.e. the O.N.C. entrants and trade entrants, and where the figures are given for one of these, the other can be obtained by subtraction from the total respondents. In addition the computer programme made it possible to analyse the four cohorts separately. The largest and most homogeneous of these was the 1957 one which consisted of O.N.C. entrants only and this has been used occasionally where it was advantageous to control the age and course of study variables.

Roughly 70 per cent of the respondents had been registered in first-year O.N.C. classes at the time of our first meeting and the remaining 30 per cent were divided fairly evenly between those who initially attended classes in mechanical trades and those in electrical trades.

The presentation of the results follows roughly the same pattern in each chapter: statistics and discussion point by point of the appropriate data, followed by individual instances (based on the interviews) by way of illustration.

CHAPTER 3

From School to Work

Our study starts with the school leaver looking for a job and the first part of the questionnaire was geared to determine first, how old he was and where he fitted into the family pattern i.e. number of children, his position in the family. Next we asked for the level of skill of his father's job, what kind of school he went to and finally how easy it was to find a job to his liking. In addition to this we already had records of test scores which gave some measure of his ability. Tables show the interaction between these variables and response rates have been calculated where possible.

Age of leaving

Nearly two-thirds of the respondents had left school by fifteen and as might be expected the later leavers were over-represented in the O.N.C. group. The difference was greater in the 1960 study as 'staying on' had by then become much more usual, and the longer the schooling the more likely, by and large, was acceptance for an O.N.C. course. Response rates could be calculated for the 1960 students as age of leaving was available on the record cards: for the sixteen-year-old leavers response was 54 per cent and for the fifteen-year-olds 32 per cent, but this was not simply an age difference as there is some interaction with the differential responses of O.N.C. and trade students which are recorded in Chapter 5, page 68.

On average this sample of part-time day-release students had reached fifteen years – the minimum school leaving age at the time of the study – between 1949 and 1959. They can be compared with the National Survey sample who reached the age of fifteen in March 1961. Approximately half the National sample left at Easter, the earliest opportunity, and a further 10 per cent at the end of the summer term, i.e. about 60 per cent,[1] compared with 63 per cent

[1] Douglas, J. W. B. et al, *All Our Future*, Peter Davies, 1968.

26

of our sample as shown in Table 3.1. The next stage of the analysis of the National sample shows that about 45 per cent of the fifteen-year-old male leavers entered some form of part-time (and in some cases full-time) further education.[1]

TABLE 3.1

Age of leaving school

Samples	Size		Age of leaving 14	15	16	17	18 and over
Total respondents	641²	N	25	381	211	19	5
	100%	%	4	59	33	3	1
Total interviewees	166	N	6	99	53	8	0
	100%	%	<4	<60	32	5	0
O.N.C. respondents	442	N	10	243	171	14	4
	100%	%	2	55	39	3	1
Trade respondents	199	N	15	138	40	5	1
	100%	%	8	69	20	>2	Trace
O.N.C. interviewees	115	N	3	62	44	6	0
	100%	%	3	54	38	5	0
Trade interviewees	51	N	3	37	9	2	0
	100%	%	6	72	18	4	0

Previous schooling

As already indicated in the Preface about two-thirds of the 2,000 subjects of this investigation had attended secondary modern schools. Comprehensive education was only just beginning in the Midlands when the last group was tested (1960). Table 3.2 shows the distribution of four samples between three types of schooling. Among the O.N.C. students 43 per cent had attended selective schools.

[1] Quoted by permission of Dr. Douglas from a privately circulated report on 'the School Leavers at Work and College'.
² Minor discrepancies in the numbers analysed can be assumed to be due to incomplete records.

TABLE 3.2

Previous schooling

Samples	Size		Selective grammar and technical	Modern	Others[1]
O.N.C. respondents	442	N	190	231	21
		%	43	52	5
Trade respondents	202	N	29	161	12
		%	14	80	6
O.N.C. interviewees	115	N	49	59	7
		%	43	51	6
Trade interviewees	51	N	7	49	2
		%	14	82	4

The identity of the interview sample with the respondent sample reflects the fact that among these subjects success in the college examinations in the early years of their learnerships showed no clear relationship with previous schooling.

207 cards had no record of previous schooling but response rates were calculated on the remaining 1944 and showed only marginal superiority for the selective school leaver as compared with those from secondary modern schools: 35 per cent and 31 per cent respectively. With over 10 per cent not known no credence can be given to such a small difference.

Table 3.3 shows that 58 per cent of all respondents and 52 per cent of those starting in O.N.C. classes left school without any kind of certificate.

Ability and personality as measured by tests

A total of seven tests (two attainment, one personality, one space perception and three cognitive) had been used in the previous researches and scores were recorded on a ten-point scale. The complex relationship between test results and success in technical college examinations, including the importance of non-intellectual factors, has been dealt with elsewhere (Venables, 1967) and will be

[1] Includes comprehensive and private school leavers and the occasional student who had attended a special school.

TABLE 3.3

Qualifications obtained before leaving school

| | | | *Qualifications* | | | | | |
| | | | None | | School leaving certificate Preliminary technical certificates e.g. U.L.C.I. | | Some 'O' Levels but not enough to qualify for the 2nd year of the O.N.C. course | |
Samples	N	%	N	%	N	%	N	%
O.N.C. respondents	442	100	229	51·8	105	23·8	108	24·4
Trade respondents	199	100	142	71·3	43	21·6	14	7·1
O.N.C. interviewees	115	100	57	49·6	29	25·2	29	25·2
Trade interviewees	49	100	27	55·1	16	32·7	6	12·2

considered here only in the broadest terms. Two simplified tables are presented below (Table 3.4 (a) and (b)) using the two tests which proved to be the best predictors in the earlier studies i.e. Raven's Matrices 1947, a non-verbal reasoning test, and Vernon's test of Arithmetic-Mathematic attainment.

The ten-point scale of scores has been reduced to two in each case, labelled low and high. The dividing lines were chosen to give the maximum differences in response rates. Raven's Matrices had been used in all four of the previous studies and the Mathematics test in three of them. On both tests there were significantly more high scorers among the respondents than among those who did not return a questionnaire, but the scores of the interview sample indicate differences between the tests. In the first case – the Matrices – the interviewees reproduce exactly the pattern of the total respondents suggesting that high and low scores were distributed randomly through the strata of successful and less successful students. On the Mathematics test the interview sample results correspond

TABLE 3.4 (a) and (b)

Response in relation to test scores

(a) Raven's Matrices

Samples	Size		Scores	
			Low	High
Respondents total[1]	584	N	226	358
		%	39	61
Non-respondents total	1302	N	649	653
		%	50	50
Total 'at risk'	1886	N	875	1011
		%	46	54
(Response rates)			26%[2]	35%[2]
Interviewees total[1]	148	N	58	90
		%	39	61
Respondents O.N.C.	401	N	119	282
		%	30	70
Interviewees O.N.C.	102	N	32	70
		%	31	69

[1] No difference between interviewees and respondents on this variable.
[2] Chi squared = 20·14 p < 0·001.

(b) Vernon's Arithmetic Mathematics test

Samples	Size	Mean age when tested		Scores	
				Low	High
Respondents total[1]	503	16·73	N	258	245
			%	51	49
Non-respondents total	1051	—	N	697	354
			%	66	34
Total 'at risk'	1554	—	N	955	599
			%	61	39
(Response rates)				27%[2]	41%[2]
Interviewees total[1]	132	16·70	N	77	55
			%	58	42
Respondents O.N.C.	355	16·77	N	141	214
			%	40	60
Interviewees O.N.C.	92	16·77	N	44	48
			%	48	52

more closely with the total at risk which is consonant with the fact that this test gave a higher correlation with first-year examination results than any other of the tests used in the earlier studies. Note also that the O.N.C. students are distinguished from the rest by higher scores, particularly on the Mathematics test.

In relation to the three tests which had been used to assess verbal intelligence – Mill Hill Vocabulary, Group Test 33 and AH_4 (which also contains a non-verbal section) – the pattern of response was similar: a slight, but in these cases insignificant, bias in favour of the higher scorers. The interviewees were biased slightly in favour of the high scores on the first two but in relation to scores on AH_4 the proportion of high scorers interviewed was exactly representative of the proportion 'at risk'. On the space perception test (Form Relations) it was the low scorers who had the higher response rate ($p = 0.001$) but the interview sample was without bias.

The only other test results available were those on the Maudsley Personality Inventory (M.P.I.) in which subjects rate themselves on a neurotic/non-neurotic continuum (the N scale) and an extraversion/introversion (E) scale. Only members of the 1960 cohort numbering

[1] Interviewees more representative of those 'at risk'.
[2] Chi squared = 32·416 p < 0·001.

460 took this test. On the N scale the less neurotic student tended to be the more responsive and on the E scale the pattern of response rates was curvilinear with greater response at the extremes. Numbers were small and differences did not reach a 'significant' level. The proportion of these technical college students scoring high on introversion (low on the E scale) was small and they were rather more reluctant to be interviewed. Partly because of this they were under-represented in the interview sample: 13 per cent instead of 18 per cent. There was no significant bias in favour of low or high scorers on the N scale among the interviewees.

Test scores in relation to schooling and family structure

On all the cognitive tests those from selective schools had, as would be expected, higher mean scores than those from the modern schools but the overlap was considerable. The small group of 'others' had in some cases higher means than the selective group. Scores on the personality test (M.P.I.) in relation to schooling tended to be the reverse of that which obtains among university students. This is explicable on the assumption that selective school children with high introversion scores are more likely to stay at school and go on to university while those who score as extraverts tend to leave early, find a job and seek their further education at the local technical college. For the secondary modern school pupil, going on to college spells academic 'success' and those who choose to do this tend to be those with higher scores at the introvert end of the scale.

Information about family size and ages of siblings relative to the respondent's age was obtained on the questionnaire which enabled us to enlarge the data available from the 1960 study. The highest mean scores on the cognitive tests were obtained by only children and members of the larger families (over three) and the lowest scorers were the younger children in small families. Assuming that in the population at large the mean scores of children in large families are lower than for those in small families,[1] this finding is consistent with the hypothesis that able boys from large families tend to seek their higher education at a technical college.

University students as a group are overweighted with only

[1] See *The Trend of Scottish Intelligence*, Scottish Council for Research in Education, 1949; and Venables and Warburton (1956) 'Relationship between the Intelligence of Technical College Students and Size of Family', *Eugenics Review*, Vol. 47, No. 4.

TABLE 3.5

Number of children in family

Sample		1		2		3		4		5		6		7		8 or more	
	N	%	N	%	N	%	N	%	N	%	N	%	N	%	N	%	N	%
Total respondents	636	100	126	20	230	36	159	25	70	11	28	4	14	2	6	1	3	1
Total O.N.C. respondents	440	100	76	17	158	36	115	26	52	12	22	5	11	2	4	1	2	1
Total interviewees	165	100	37	22	65	39	42	25	14	8	4	3	1	1	1	1	1	1

children, first-borns, members of small families and those rating themselves on the M.P.I. tests as 'neurotic' and 'introverted'. The 'only children' in this sample had higher mean scores on extraversion than the others and rated themselves as less neurotic. It is possible that among such children personality is a more important factor in the choice whether to leave school and start work or to continue in full-time education, than it is for children in large families where the economic implications of the choice are likely to have a greater impact.

The lowest mean scores on the E scale i.e. those rating themselves at the 'introversion' end, were the younger sons in families of two and those in the middle position. The younger sons, especially those with an older sister, were the highest scorers on the N scale.

It should be emphasised that these young engineers as a whole ranked as less 'neurotic' and more 'extraverted' than the general population.

Social class by father's occupation

Subjects were asked to state their father's job as explicitly as possible and in tabulating the responses we were able to use the seven-point scale of skill level devised by Mr. David Nelson for the National Survey. Differences are in the expected direction with O.N.C. entrants having a higher proportion of professionally qualified fathers and fewer semi- and unskilled workers. Just over half of each group had fathers in highly skilled and skilled jobs. Differences between total respondents and the interview samples indicate a lower response rate from ex-students whose fathers were in categories 5 and 6. This finding is interrelated with the bias in favour of college success.

Categories 1 and 2 are shown separately in Table 3.6 but are recorded together in subsequent ones as no certainty can be attached to the rating of the nine fathers (eight O.N.C. and one Trade) as Higher Professional (see Nelson's Classification, Appendix II, page 163). They were listed (by their sons) as directors of firms, qualified engineers and – in one case – accountant. If the firms they directed were small (as some were agreed to be during interviews) and if the 'qualified' engineers were not in fact of chartered status and if the 'accountant' was also not 'chartered' then the nine should join the sixty-nine in category 2 Lower Professional.

TABLE 3.6

Social class by father's occupation

Father's job	O.N.C. Respondents		Trade respondents		O.N.C. interviewees		Trade interviewees	
	N	%	N	%	N	%	N	%
1. Professional	8	2	1	Trace	4	4	1	2
2. Lower Professional	56	13	13	7	11	10	1	2
3. Highly Skilled	127	30	59	33	24	23	16	34
4. Skilled	105	25	32	18	28	26+	7	15
5. Moderately Skilled	79	19	44	24	28	26+	12	26
6. Semi- and Unskilled	44	11	32	18	11	10	10	21
	419	100	181	100	106	100	47	100

Information on fathers' jobs was also available for 556 of the non-respondents and followed a very similar pattern. The proportions shown in Table 3.6 follow very closely those given in *The Young Worker at College* for the 1960 cohort.[1]

Table 3.7 shows the interrelation between the level of father's job and the previous schooling of his son. The proportions 43 per cent selective schools, 52 per cent modern among O.N.C. students are reflected at each skill level with statistically insignificant differences. The local tech. has tended to be seen as a place for the training of working-class youth but it is in fact also used by professional families whose children either leave the grammar or technical school early or fail to reach a selective school. The figures for the interview samples do not differ significantly from the total samples confirming that early success at college is unrelated to the parents' job level.

We now have a picture of our subjects as school leavers: early leavers from selective schools working alongside modern school pupils accepted for O.N.C. courses (often after a year in a preliminary class). Three quarters of them had fathers in skilled jobs, many of them in engineering industries.

So we turn to the question of finding a job. At the end of the questionnaire they were asked to look back on the years between

[1] Ibid., p. 73.

TABLE 3.7

School by level of father's job

| | | Father's job level | | | | | | | | |
| | | Professional | | Highly Skilled | | Skilled | | Moderately, Semi- and Unskilled | | Totals | |
Samples	Schools	N	%	N	%	N	%	N	%	N	%
O.N.C. respondents	Selective	26	40·6	49	38·3	47	45·2	59	48·0	181	43·2
	Modern	32	50·0	72	56·2	53	51·0	60	48·8	217	51·8
	Other	6	9·4	7	5·5	4	3·8	4	3·2	21	5·0
	Totals	64	100·0	128	100·0	104	100·0	123	100·0	419	100·0
Trade respondents	Selective	3	21·4	6	10·3	5	17·2	7	9·2	21	11·9
	Modern	10	71·4	49	84·5	23	79·3	65	85·5	147	85·0
	Other	1	7·2	3	5·2	1	3·5	4	5·3	9	5·1
	Totals	14	100·0	58	100·0	29	100·0	76	100·0	177	100·0
O.N.C. interviewees	Selective	5	33·3	9	37·5	13	46·4	18	46·2	45	42·4
	Modern	9	60·0	14	58·3	13	46·4	19	48·7	55	51·9
	Other	1	6·7	1	4·2	2	7·2	2	5·1	6	5·7
	Totals	15	100·0	24	100·0	28	100·0	39	100·0	106	100·0
Trade interviewees	Selective	1	50·0	2	13·3	1	14·3	2	9·5	6	13·3
	Modern	0	0	13	86·7	5	71·4	19	90·5	37	82·3
	Other	1	50·0	0	0	1	14·3	0	0	2	4·5
	Totals	2	100·0	15	100·0	7	100·0	21	100·0	45	100·0

leaving school and becoming an adult worker and say how they felt about the opportunities open to them when they were looking for their first employment. They were offered five ratings from 'Very satisfactory' to 'Very poor' and those who felt satisfied were asked to say why. The results are set out in Tables 3.8, 3.9 and 3.10 using column percentages.

Row percentages are given in Appendix III, Tables A3.8 and A3.9, pages 168–69. In Table 3.8 49 per cent ($\frac{206}{417}$) of the O.N.C. respondents used one of the two satisfactory ratings and 58 per cent of the trade entrants who responded ($\frac{107}{184}$). The probability that

TABLE 3.8

Opportunities for finding a job in relation to schooling

Column percentages

Sample	Schools	Very satisfactory and satisfactory		Fair		Poor and very poor		Totals	
		N^1	%	N	%	N	%	N	%
O.N.C. respondents	Selective	103	50·0	50	37·3	26	33·8	179	42·9
	Modern	95	46·1	75	56·0	49	63·6	219	52·5
	Other	8	3·9	9	6·7	2	2·6	19	4·6
	Totals	206	100·0	134	100·0	77	100·0	417²	100·0
O.N.C. interviewees	Selective	29	53·7	10	27·8	8	38·1	47	42·3
	Modern	23	42·6	22	61·1	13	61·9	58	52·3
	Other	2	3·7	4	11·1	0		6	5·4
	Totals	54	100·0	36	100·0	21	100·0	111	100·0
Trade respondents	Selective	13	12·1	3	6·1	5	17·9	21	11·4
	Modern	90	84·1	42	85·7	23	82·1	155	84·2
	Other	4	3·8	4	8·2	0		8	4·4
	Totals	107	100·0	49	100·0	28	100·0	184²	100·0
Trade interviewees	Selective	6	19·4	0	—	1	16·7	7	14·3
	Modern	23	74·2	12	100·0	5	83·3	40	81·6
	Other	2	6·4	0	—	0	—	2	4·1
	Totals	31	100·0	12	100·0	6	100·0	49	100·0

[1] Roughly one-third of the totals in this column were in the 'Very satisfactory' category.
[2] 26 of the O.N.C. group (6%) and 17 of the trade (8%) did not answer this question.

TABLE 3.9

Opportunities for finding a job in relation to level of father's job

Column percentages

Samples	Level of job	Very satisfactory and satisfactory		Fair		Poor and very poor		Totals	
		N	%	N	%	N	%	N	%
	Professional	30	15·4	23	18·3	7	10·0	60	15·3
	Highly								
O.N.C.	Skilled	56	28·7	41	32·5	24	34·3	121	31·0
respon-	Skilled	45	23·1	34	27·0	16	22·8+	95	24·3
dents	Moderately,								
	Semi- and								
	Unskilled	64	32·8	28	22·2	23	32·8+	115	29·4
	Totals	195	100·0	126	100·0	70	100·0	391[1]	100·0
	Professional	8	16·0	6	18·2	1	5·3	15	14·7
	Highly								
O.N.C.	Skilled	10	20·0	6	18·2	8	42·1	24	23·5
inter-	Skilled	13	26·0	12	36·3	3	15·8	28	27·5
viewees	Moderately,								
	Semi- and								
	Unskilled	19	38·0	9	27·3	7	36·8	35	34·3
	Totals	50	100·0	33	100·0	19	100·0	102	100·0
	Professional	11	11·5	0	0	1	4·0	12	7·1
	Highly								
Trade	Skilled	27	28·1	19	40·4	9	36·0	55	32·7
respon-	Skilled	22	22·9	3	6·4	3	12·0	28	16·7
dents	Moderately,								
	Semi and								
	Unskilled	36	37·5	25	53·2	12	48·0	73	43·5
	Totals	96	100·0	47	100·0	25	100·0	168[1]	100·0
	Professional	2	6·7	0	0	0	0	2	4·4
	Highly								
Trade	Skilled	12	40·0	2	18·2	0	0	14	31·1
inter-	Skilled	7	23·3	0	0	0	0	7	15·6
viewees	Moderately,								
	Semi- and								
	Unskilled	9	30·0	9	81·8	4	100·0	22	48·9
	Totals	30	100·0	11	100·0	4	100·0	45	100·0

[1] Information was incomplete for 52 O.N.C. respondents (12%) and 33 of the trade (16%).

this result arose by chance is 1 in 20. Satisfaction is partly a function of expectation and it is not unlikely that those accepted for O.N.C. courses have higher expectations about their job opportunities than the others and are consequently less satisfied with the reality.

Comparing percentages in the totals column with comparable figures in the others the direction of differences can be readily detected. For example in Table 3.8 in every sub-sample under Column 1 (Very satisfactory and Satisfactory) the percentages related to the selective school leavers is higher than the percentage for the totals column, whereas for the modern school group it is lower. For the larger (O.N.C.) group the difference was significant at the 1 in 100 level but numbers in the trade group were too small to show a dependable level of significance.

Turning to Table 3.9, the responses of those whose fathers had 'professional' jobs can be compared with those of sons of skilled workers.

In the O.N.C. group the proportion rating themselves satisfied was around 50 per cent at each level of skill with the least skilled group the most satisfied ($\frac{64}{115} = 56$ per cent).[1] Among the trade students the trend is reversed: 11 of the 12 sons in the 'professional' group declared themselves satisfied and the proportion of 'satisfactory' ratings was least among the least skilled group ($\frac{36}{73} = 49$ per cent).

Asking for ratings on a 'Satisfaction' scale is obvious enough, but interpreting the answers is far from straightforward. In the first place job satisfaction is related to expectations, as has already been mentioned, and also to self-image and self-evaluation. For the interview sample some assessment of these factors was possible and among the rest comments on the questionnaire occasionally gave a clue. In a large number of cases, and this was particularly true of the trade sample, opportunities were considered to be 'satisfactory' if the school leaver got a job at all. These students as a group tend to be realists: they do not generally entertain high ambitions: they have little truck with fantasy.

The seven thumb-nail sketches which follow relate to the seven trade interviewees from selective schools who figure in the right-hand column of Table 3.8, page 37. They are based on questionnaire responses and interview discussions. The two sons of directors of small firms are included among them in paragraphs 1 and 4 respectively. The age in 1966 when the interviews took place is given first.

1. Aged thirty-four. Technical school. Only son of a director of a

[1] See Appendix III, Table A3.9, p. 169 for row percentages.

small electrical firm. Wanted to learn the job but hadn't a great deal of time for day release. Better in his own time at night school – 'too much messing about in the day time'. Now a co-director and begrudges day release for his employees which ceases firmly at eighteen. Resents the Industrial Training Act. Confesses himself 'envious of those chaps with university degrees' and thought that if he won a fortune on the pools he'd 'give everything up and go to the university'.

2. Aged thirty-two. An only child – father died when he was very young; he, the father, had had 'no regular job prior to his death'. 'Never liked school – only too anxious to leave. Some of the discipline seemed pointless.' Explaining 'why' he was 'satisfied' he wrote, 'I have an interesting and worthwhile job with good conditions and prospects. However, had I started studying for O.N.C. and H.N.C. earlier I would have had more opportunities.' He had remained with the electrical firm where he had been trained, and had risen to become an 'assistant engineer'. He discussed his career and his promotion prospects in detail during the interview. 'Very difficult to leave the longer you stay – mainly because of the pension scheme which is non-contributory.' Of his grammar-school education – early leaving and part-time education he thought that nowadays a chap like him would take 'A' levels and then do a sandwich course to become a qualified electrical engineer. He had started the O.N.C. course in 1960, ten years after his first year in the trade course which he completed satisfactorily five years later. This he felt had been a false start for a grammar-school leaver. 'In studying at the Tech. and trying to get qualifications there's a conflict between the present job and the next one.' He had experienced this himself and now as a manager responsible for some of the trainees he was very aware of it. 'Advanced technical work and understanding not all that relevant to me now.' And he had no training for management. He enjoyed part-time teaching at the Tech. and would like to do more but financial prospects better if he stays.

3. Aged thirty. Rated himself very satisfied. 'I had every opportunity to enter almost any trade I wished.' First grammar-school child in family of seven children – 'financially difficult'. 'I was "hot headed" – thought of the present not the future. At school you can't see the financial rewards of staying on.' Mother wanted him to stay on which would have been a struggle. 'I was very independent and wanted to do the struggling myself.' Three older brothers, two in engineering trades. Father a lorry driver. Regrets the decision now.

'Did not think then of all the levels and the variety of work.' 'It was entirely my own fault.'

4. Aged twenty-four. Minor public school – father managing director of a small family business. He and number 1 above are the two 'trade' students in Table 3.9 with fathers in the 'professional' class. Numbers 4, 5 and 6 of these sketches were subjects of the 1960 researches and this young man appeared as Mark Friedlander in *The Young Worker at College*.[1] By the age of twenty-four he had travelled abroad working for his father on the sales side and was now in charge of a special department of the firm. He was 'satisfied' with the job opportunity of being able to carry on his father's business, but he was still unable to spell. He still enjoyed being a craftsman and showed me examples of recent small new products for which he had himself made the prototypes.

5. Aged twenty-three. Grammar school. Father manual worker and 'definitely ambitious for me – wanted me to be labelled "staff" '. Mother also wanted him to have a greater sense of security than his parents had had. As a lad he'd wanted money and would say 'I'm going to the Austins to work nights' but it was always 'me father who talked me out of it. And I respected his opinion – it was the way I'd been brought up.' Enjoyed some things at school including Maths, but was 'a bit of a rebel' and determined to leave early. His father didn't object. But he wasn't going to be 'stuck inside four walls', wanted a trade and wanted to be outdoors. So at first became a trainee with the G.P.O. 'one place where father didn't come into it'. Later changed his job to 'try four walls and see what good I would be as a pen-pusher'. An outgoing person and a good sportsman, he now has a very good job with an American firm in a country town in the Midlands. Trained on the job and on a variety of special short courses (in the firm's time) on such topics as 'Production and Inventory Planning' and 'Computers'. Very happy and full of zest: he and his wife always wanted to live in the country. 'You're appraised once every six months here but it's acceptable. You can hit back and feel it's fair. Very exciting atmosphere. I have faith in this company – they promote on objective grounds and they have a very satisfied work force. But you grow grey early – can't cope with the pressure – so you're put out to grass early.' His rating of 'very satisfactory' for his job opportunities was 'due to the varied opportunities offered by the industries in Birmingham'.

6. Aged twenty-three. Grammar school. Father a toolmaker. Left

[1] p. 58.

school at fifteen 'which was a stupid thing to do'. Very much regretted it. He followed his father into an engineering trade and took no interest in the college classes because he was merely marking time until he could join the police force. 'I'm now completely in favour of education – realised it at nineteen as soon as I joined the force.' He was 'very satisfied' with his job opportunities 'because for every interview I attended I was accepted and consequently I had no difficulty in obtaining a job'. However he 'would not allow him [his son, when he has one] to discontinue his studies as I was allowed to'. Thoroughly enjoying his new life including the study. 'I hate routine – going to work in the same bus each morning.' Likes shift work – socially chaotic – but he thinks he sees more of his wife. He thinks *Z Cars* influenced him very much but he has no regrets. 'The reasons I now like the job are not the same as I had for joining – though the TV is true to life.' 'It was the glamour to be perfectly honest.' There is much more responsibility than he expected and he likes it 'but if I'd known all I would have been scared stiff'.

7. Apart from the public-school boy (Number 4), all the trade students discussed above had left their selective schools at fifteen or sixteen. The one remaining, aged thirty-four, who considered his opportunities had been poor, had stayed on at a grammar school until the age of seventeen. His father was a semi-skilled worker and his mother a district nurse. 'I found "A" levels very hard going – didn't like studying but I was then at a bit of a dead loss.' Most of his eight School Certificate passes were in Arts subjects and there was 'nothing in that line' he fancied. He settled for the G.P.O. because he couldn't get a job that he wanted. He felt he ought to have had 'more guidance earlier in school life as to which job you would be likely to do well in'. 'I'd already done all the theoretical work they were teaching at the college in Physics at the grammar school. I failed because I took it too easy.' 'You have to have an aptitude for study.' Mother had wanted him to be a doctor but at school you had to choose between Chemistry and French and 'I was top in French and a lad of twelve doesn't know what subjects to take.' His scores on the two intelligence tests were in each case above the mean for university students. In speech and manner he identified himself as 'working class'. 'No good trying to make yerself do something beyond yer – I'd rather be 'appy and 'ave me wife 'appy.' Which is fine if you really *are* happy.

Returning now to the questionnaire the satisfied respondents were asked to say why and their replies are set out in Table 3.10. The

TABLE 3.10

Comments on job opportunities

		Samples						
	Total respondents		Total interviewees		O.N.C. respondents		O.N.C. interviewees	
Type of comment	N	%	N	%	N	%	N	%
Easy: good careers talks at school (1)	8	2·4	3	3·1	5	2·3	2	3·2
Wanted industrial job and happy with it (2)	50	14·9	6	6·3	30	13·9	3	4·8
No difficulty; Youth Employment Office helpful (3)	134	40·0	39	40·6	81	37·5	28	44·4
Ambitions fulfilled (4)	13	3·9	8	8·3	7	3·2	4	6·3
Plenty of opportunities – up to the individual (5)	90	26·9	28	29·2	65	30·1	17	27·0
School no help (6)	4	1·2	3	3·1	2	0·9	2	3·2
Youth Employment Office no help (7)	23	6·9	5	5·2	16	7·4	3	4·8
Schooling a waste of time (8)	4	1·2	2	2·1	4	1·9	2	3·2
No choice – had to take what he could get (9)	9	2·7	2	2·1	6	2·8	2	3·2
Totals	335	100·1	96	100·0	216	100·0	63	100·1

numbers between this and the preceding tables do not tally exactly as some people who had rated their opportunities only 'fair' also added comments.

Some respondents – about 12 per cent – took the opportunity to add negative comments indicating that although they had found a job to their liking this reflected no credit on the school or Youth Employment Officer. However, at least 300 of the 644 erstwhile engineering apprentices who replied to the questionnaire looked back with satisfaction to their transfer from school to work and 20 per cent chose, without prompting, to pay a tribute to the Youth Employment Officer. There were no significant differences between O.N.C. students and the rest.

One of the two topics on which specific information was elicited during the interviews was concerned with this question of how the transfer from school to work had been made and under what circumstances. How did they decide when to leave and what work to do and what part did their parents and teachers play? How – looking back – did they now feel about it all? Notes taken on the spot were subsequently analysed under eight headings. Although based on recorded statements the selection is inevitably a subjective one. The differences between rating scale results and impressions obtained in a long open-ended interview are always interesting and often important. Table 3.11 summarises the results.

In using the rating scale they had concentrated on the actual mechanics of finding a job, but in conversation they were much more inclined to ruminate about why they had chosen to leave school early and to express regrets that they had set their sights so low. Also in many cases they could do no other and as men in their twenties and thirties they were prepared to look back fairly calmly at the family circumstances which had restricted their freedom of choice. Such discussion led naturally to consideration of their hopes for their own children which are discussed more fully in Chapter 7.

Two examples follow, illustrative of the two largest of the eight groups – names are changed as well as some inessential details.

Fred Easterby was an only child, had attended a central school and done 'very well in the school examinations'. Both intelligence test scores obtained in the first year of an O.N.C. course were high with verbal ability better than non-verbal which was unusual. The verbal score placed him in the same range as the top 30 per cent of university students. He could have taken the School Certificate examination but he left school at fifteen and a half. 'Most of us left. When you

TABLE 3.11

From school to work

Assessments based on information obtained in the interviews	N	%
1. Successful group who looked back with satisfaction. Ambitious. Keen to start work. One-sixth of this group (6 persons) could be classified as 'over-achievers'. Scores suggested only very modest ability and good support from interested adults was probably an essential ingredient in their success.	36	22
2. Not very successful. Lack of drive or wish to study. Family emphasised security. Father dead or ill. Some family pressures often from the mother who had had a better education than the father. Felt they 'could have done better'. Talk of a 'misspent youth'.	15	9
3. Regretted leaving school early. Not interested in studying at school. Too many other interests. Regretted not going to a grammar school. Had wanted their 'independence'. 'Thought of the present rather than the future', and had not had enough encouragement either from parents or school.	17	10
4. Father had 'insisted on a trade'. Wanted him to have a better job and a better life than he [father] had had. Father keen on qualifications. Saw himself as following in father's footsteps. Ambitious. Self-confident. Knew what he wanted and persisted until he found the right job.	26	16
5. Special circumstances. Early leaving inevitable. Unable to do as he wished. Widowed mother. Eldest of large family. Family illness. Over-protected, only son. Nervous about examinations. Homework and reports better than examination results. O.N.C. too big a jump from a secondary modern school.	16	9+
6. Undecided. Badly advised. Transfer from school to work 'not easy', 'chancy'. No college nearby. Difficulties in attending college. Dissatisfied with first firm. Changes of job. Not able to get what he really wanted.	30	18
7. Drop-outs. College work too difficult. No interest in academic side of the job. Dissatisfied with firm. No help in choosing a job. Going to work 'a shock'. More interested in social life, sport. Regrets.	15	9
8. Drifting. Unsettled. Very glad to leave school. Rebelled against parents and/or teachers. Threat of National Service. Some of this group reported improved attitudes to study after National Service.	11	6+
Total	166	100

come from a working class home you're not advised properly.' He greatly regretted leaving early. His father was a labourer and found him a job in the same firm: 'I wanted to be an electrician but they only needed an apprentice fitter.' 'Being an inquisitive type' he said he had taught himself to some extent and tried various jobs. He 'went on the knocker' (became a salesman) for six weeks ... 'soul-destroying irregular hours, hopeless for family life' ... 'But it was well worth it – taught me a lot about people.'

When interviewed he was thirty-four, married with two children, and working as a maintenance engineer for the local authority. He was 'fairly content' with the job he had, but complained about the level of pay.

He had passed the first year of the O.N.C. but failed in the second year because he didn't sit all the examinations. He had done no further college study of any consequence. 'When you get to the age of realising what these things mean you're too old to take it up again. You're too fixed with a wife and children.' On the questionnaire answered in his first year at college he wrote of his ambition for 'managerial work: an office where you can use your own initiative'. In replying to the follow-up questionnaire he rated his opportunities for finding a job as 'very poor' and his works training as 'unsatisfactory' adding by way of comment 'this seems to be the normal way of learning a trade except in very large firms'.

He and his wife were very keenly involved in their children's schooling and took a leading part in several community activities – tenants association, parent-teachers, adventure playgrounds and so on. His children he said 'will stay at school till eighteen and go on to get as many qualifications as they can'. Here his wife, who had had a better education then he, joined in to endorse what he was saying. He was scathing about part-time education: 'One day a week! ... You've forgotten what the hell you did the week before. And if you're on your own as I was [small firm, only O.N.C. apprentice] you've no chance to discuss it.' He went on to discuss his family background: 'attitude to schooling is a "family thing" ... working men feel cut off from it [e.g. his father] ... it's a closed world they know nothing about. And we had no parent-teacher association then.'

Mr. Easterby's account of his transfer from school to work is an example from category 6 of Table 3.11. The second example is the extreme case from category 1.

Martin Steel was twenty-five when interviewed married with one child. He had attended a secondary modern school had one older brother and his father was a fitter. He was one of the 1957 sample each of whom was in a first-year O.N.C. class when first contacted. Boys from his school sat the preliminary technical examinations set by the Union of Engineering Institutions (U.E.I.) for the first time in 1956. He passed in all the subjects and left school at Easter, starting work as an apprentice with one of the Midland car firms in the following September. 'I had a full term's holiday – the last one you get for a long time.' His father wanted him to go to a private school to take 'O' and 'A' levels and then go on to University. 'He didn't really want me to be an engineer – he's a thinker – assessing the supply and demand situation. 'Go into a profession' he said. He suggested architecture and persuaded me to write after a job in an architect's office and I was offered it.' But Martin had his lathe and all his tools and from his earliest days these were what had interested him.

His college career was a rare success story. In the first three years he not only obtained an O.N.C. in Mechanical Engineering but passes in four G.C.E. subjects and the Intermediate Examination of the City and Guilds. He chose his firm because of their training scheme and he stayed because 'they allow you to continue training'. 'There's a great difference between getting a job in order to earn a living and those who take a job in order to be trained for it.'

IIe was given block release in order to do the Higher National Diploma in Mechanical and Production Engineering rather than the Certificate course and 'didn't find it easy'. He had no failures and he was just twenty-one when he passed the final examination. 'This was where my father was right – if I'd studied up to 'A' level I'd have found it easier.'

He was still continuing with his studies taking various courses at the local university in Works Management and related subjects with a view to an Associateship eventually. He had just returned from four months' full-time on a postgraduate specialist course at one of the northern universities which he had greatly enjoyed. 'Some lectures but mainly left to yourself with plenty of guidance. Quite different from the Tech.' Had been on the point of leaving his firm but as a result of the specialist course had been promoted to the relevant research department. 'Came out of the blue – made me realise I hadn't been forgotten.'

Looking back he said he didn't know why he had failed the 11+, he'd always been in the top of the 'A' stream. 'I suppose I didn't apply myself till I was thirteen or fourteen which in the present educational system is too late.' 'But it was anyway early enough for me to avoid being out there as a fitter' (reference to his luck in being able to take the U.E.I. examinations). 'Comprehensive schools will score here – natural selection.' 'The demand now is for a different type of engineer – things are changing. People used to say "it's not what you know but who you know" – it's not so true now.' Engineers, he said, need academic knowledge to use as a tool as well as practical experience. They are dealing with people and this requires a broader education – dealing with the human aspects – 'wrong assessments [of people] by a supervisor can cost a lot of money.'

In my 1957 research,[1] in which this student was involved, the subjects were given verbal and other tests on entry and took them again in their third year at college. Changes in scores were calculated for the 'successful' group who had had no failures in the first two examinations and for the remaining (relatively) unsuccessful group. Gains on the verbal test averaged 20 points for the former and 13 for the latter. Mr. Steel's first verbal score put him in the bottom 50 per cent of the population and was low enough to explain his 11+ failure. His second one fell into the range of the top 25 per cent. The gain was among the largest recorded: 26·5 points as against an average of 14·1. His non-verbal score which was unchanged over the two- to three-year period was at the mean for university students. The only examination he had ever failed was G.C.E. English – twice. In his fifth year he took a special English course, 'spent more time reading', and passed. 'I'll put this right with my boy' was his parting shot.

[1] Venables, E., 'Changes in Intelligence Test Scores of Engineering Apprentices between the First and Third Years of Attendance at College', *Brit. J. Educational Psychology*, 1961, Vol. XXXI, Part III, pp. 257–64.

CHAPTER 4

Serving their Time: Training within the Firm

In Section II of the questionnaire the erstwhile apprentices were asked about their first jobs, the kinds of firms which recruited them, what they thought of the works training they received and what jobs they had held once their training was completed. The replies are collated in Tables 4.1 to 4.10.

The first employers were analysed according to whether they were manufacturers, contractors or public bodies and the manufacturing organisations were further broken down by scale of production. In the 1957 and 1960 studies the size of the firms in terms of numbers of employees had been recorded so it was possible to calculate response rates in relation to size for these two sub-samples (Table 4.1). No question was asked about size on the questionnaire since answers from the older cohorts (1950 and 1952) were unlikely to be reliable after such a lapse of time.

Large firms are over-represented in part-time day-release classes and in the respondent sample shown in Table 4.1 those from large firms comprised 53 per cent of the whole ($\frac{225}{418}$). Among the total at risk, students from large firms numbered 50 per cent ($\frac{483}{971}$). The response rate from those initially apprenticed to large firms was significantly greater than it was from those in firms with less than 100 employees, but not significantly different from those in groups II or III. Among the interview sample 54 per cent were from the largest firms chiefly because those on block-release courses who were added to the sample were mainly from such firms.

Most subsequent tables deal with the total respondent sample. Two-thirds of them had spent their apprenticeship years in manufacturing industry concerned with various types of product. The rest were employed in contracting firms or by public bodies such as Local Authorities and the Post Office. The types of employing firm (Table 4.2) were remarkably similar for the four samples both over the years 1950 to 1960 and geographically as between the North-West

49

TABLE 4.1

Response rates by size of firm

1957 and 1960 sub-samples only

| | | Size of firm by number of employees | | | | |
		I 99 and below	II 100–249	III 250–999	IV 1000+	Totals
Respondents		**61**	**50**	**82**	**225**	**418**
	Response rates	33%	46%	42%	47%	43%
Non-respondents		125	58	112	258	553
Total at risk		186	108	194	483	971
	Row percentages	19	11	20	50	100
Interview sample		**18**	**15**	**18**	**60**	**111**
	Row percentages	16	14	16	54	100
Interview sample: O.N.C.		**11**	**7**	**12**	**47**	**77**
	Row percentages	14	9	16	61	100
Interview sample: Trade		**7**	**8**	**6**	**13**	**34**
	Row percentages	>20	<24	18	38	100

Response rates I/IV   Chi squared $\left(\frac{61}{125}\big/\frac{225}{258}\right)$ = 10·4   p < 0·001

and the Midlands. The figures for the random sample follow the same pattern suggesting that the respondents are representative of those at risk in relation to early employment. The detailed figures for the interview sample indicate a somewhat higher proportion of trade students among the respondents from contracting firms (mainly electrical) and proportionately fewer from manufacturing industries.

Within manufacturing industries (Table 4.3) regional differences are reflected in the student body. The Birmingham samples contain a high proportion of workers on mass production (cars, for example) and among the Manchester students more are employed on 'one-offs' (e.g. large turbines). This bias is not correctly reflected in the interview sample because the two regions were not sampled equally i.e. only 5 per cent of the Manchester group was drawn as against 10 per cent from the Midlands. Again the differences between O.N.C. and Trade respondents (final column) are small with proportionately more trade students engaged in large batch production.

TABLE 4.2
(For details see Appendix III, Table A4.2, page 170)

Distribution of respondents according to type of first employment as apprentices

	All respondents						Interview sample			
	Man-chester sample		Birming-ham sample		Totals		Totals		O.N.C. only	
Type of employing firm	N	%	N	%	N	%	N	%	N	%
Manufacturing firms	158	72	307	73	465	73	122	74	88	77
Contracting firms	36	>16	65	>15	101	>15	22	>13	11	10
Public Bodies	24	11	47	11	71	11	20	12	14	12
Others	1	<1	2	<1	3	<1	1	<1	1	1
Grand total	219	100	421	100	640	100	165	100	114	100

85 per cent had the word 'apprentice' in their job titles: other designations were Trainee, Youth in Training, Toolmaker: just over half were actually indentured apprentices (Table 4.4). Those recruited as apprentice draughtsmen were, with only the odd exception, enrolled in O.N.C. classes. The figures indicate that they were probably under-represented among the respondents.

51

TABLE 4.3

Distribution of student workers in manufacturing industries according to scale of production

Scale of production	Manchester 1950–52 N	%	Birmingham 1957–60 N	%	Totals N	%	Interview sample Totals N	%	O.N.C. only N	%
(a) One-off	65	41	102	33	167	36	48	40	36	41
(b) Large batch	40	25	59	19	99	21	23	19	13	15
(c) Mass production	27	17	96	31	123	26	34	>28	27	31
(d) Continuous flow	4	3	12	4	16	3	5	4	3	3
(e) Other	22	14	38	13	60	14	10	>8	9	10
Totals	158	100	307	99+	465	100	120 (2NK[1])	100	88	100

TABLE 4.4

Nature of learnership

a) *Title*

Title of learnership	All respondents N	%	Interview sample Totals N	%	O.N.C. only N	%
Apprentice	242	>40	58	37	45	41
Trade apprentice	163	27	42	26	17	>15
Craft apprentice	10	<2	2	1	1	1
Apprentice draughtsman	96	16	28	18	28	>25
Total 'apprentices'	511	85	130	82	91	83
Trainee	40	>7	12	8	8	7
Youth in training	29	5	11	7	7	6
Toolmaker	17	3	4	>2	3	3
Junior technical illustrator	1	Trace	1	1	1	1
Total responding	598	100	158	100	110	100
	(NK 46)		(NK 8)		(NK 5)	

[1] NK = not known.

52

b) *Indentures*

	All respondents		Interview sample			
			Totals		O.N.C. only	
	N	%	N	%	N	%
Indentured[1]	337	53	79	48	56	49
	(5 broken)					
Not indentured	297	47	86	52	58	51
Total	634	100	165	100	114	100
	(NK 10)		(NK 1)		(NK 1)	

Questions on the training given by the firms covered its location, who was responsible, length of time and the student's opinion of its quality. The answers showed wide variation: 28 per cent had been trained in a training school and over a third 'at the bench'. For about 26 per cent of the respondents there had been a full-time instructor responsible. Over 80 per cent had had some form of works training for more than a year, though figures for the interview sample suggest that this is an overestimate, and 58 per cent of them considered that the arrangements were very good or fairly good.

At the other extreme 44 per cent of these trainees had been 'trained' by an 'older worker' and 18 per cent (an underestimate judging by the

TABLE 4.5

Question: Where did you receive your works training?

Replies	All respondents		Interview sample			
			Totals		O.N.C. only	
	N	%	N	%	N	%
(Mainly) Works training school[2]	180	28	47	28	32	28
At the bench	232	36	57	34	36	31
Throughout the works	103	16	29	18	20	>17
(Mainly) Drawing office	46	7	16	10[3]	16	14
On site and field work	57	9	13	8	7	6
No special training	26	4	4	2	4	>3
Totals	647	100	166	100	115	100

[1] Differences not significant. Chi sq. = 2·49.
[2] Includes those trained 'in part of workshop set aside for training'.
[3] Draughtsmen all in O.N.C. classes and probably under-represented among the respondents.

53

interview sample) said that there had been no one person with particular responsibility for their training. 12 per cent (N = 79) had had periods varying from no more than a year to only a few weeks in training and 134 of them (22 per cent) thought their works training had been 'rather poor' or 'unsatisfactory'. For the O.N.C. interviewees the proportion reached 28 per cent.

Opinion on the quality of the training was monitored in two ways – first on a five-point scale ranging from 'very good' through 'moderate' to 'unsatisfactory' (Table 4.8), and secondly by an open-ended request for comments. These were subsequently classified under eight heads as shown in Table 4.9. Rather more than half of the

TABLE 4.6

Question: By whom was the training given?

Replies	All respondents		Interview sample			
			Totals		O.N.C. only	
	N	%	N	%	N	%
1. Mainly by a full-time instructor	167	26	46	28	32	28
2. Supervisor	80	12	15	9	11	10
3. Older worker	284	44	69	41	44	38
4. No one particular person	113	18	36	22	28	24
Totals	644	100	166	100	115	100

TABLE 4.7

Question: How long did the training last?

Replies	All respondents		Interview sample			
			Totals		O.N.C. only	
	N	%	N	%	N	%
1. More than one year	532[1]	83	132[1]	79	88[1]	>76
2. Up to a year	23	4	8	5	7	6
3. Up to six months	40	6	9	5	7	6
4. A few weeks only	16	2	6	4	3	>2
5. No set time	33	5	11	7	10	9
Totals	644	100	166	100	115	100

[1] 106 (16·5%) of all respondents, 10 (6%) of the total interview sample and 4 (3·5%) of the O.N.C. interviewees indicated that their works training had lasted for five years.

respondents ticked the 'very good' or 'fairly good' categories ranging from 58 per cent for all respondents to 51 per cent for the O.N.C. interviewees. On the 'very good' rating O.N.C. entrants were significantly different from the craft entrants, the probability that the result was due to chance being less than one in fifty. Similarly when making comments on the works training (Table 4.9), the evidence is that the trade entrants were more favourably disposed.

TABLE 4.8

Question: What did you think of the works training you received?

	Responses on a given 5-point scale						
	Very good	Fairly good	Mod- erate	Rather poor	Un- satis- factory	Total replying	No answer
All respondents	**144**	**219**	**124**	**75**	**59**	**621**	**23**
							(3·6% of
Row percentages	23	35	20	12	10	100	644)
O.N.C. respondents	**85**	**156**	**91**	**57**	**38**	**427**	**16**
							(3·6% of
Row percentages	20	37	21	13	9	100	443)
All interviewees	**34**	**53**	**31**	**19**	**23**	**160**	**6**
							(3·6% of
Row percentages	21	33	19	12	14	100	166)
O.N.C. interviewees	**17**	**39**	**23**	**16**	**14**	**109**	**6**
							(5·2% of
Row percentages	15	36	21	15	13	100	115)

	Very good to Moderate	Rather poor Unsatis- factory	Totals
Interviewed	**118**	**42**	**160**
Row percentages	74	26	100
Not interviewed	**369**	**92**	**461**
Row percentages	80	20	100
Totals	**487**	**134**	**621**
Row percentages	78	22	100

Chi sq. $= 2·78$ p $= 0·1$

Interview sample representing all those at risk made a smaller proportion of favourable ratings on their works training than the respondent sample which was overweighted with students successful in their college studies. Probability that this was due to chance 1 in 10. Analysis for O.N.C. respondents only gives a similar result.

	'Very good' rating	All others	Totals
O.N.C. interviewees	17	92	109
Trade interviewees	17	34	51
Totals	34	126	160

Chi sq. $= 6 \cdot 2$ $p < 0 \cdot 02$

Results for the interview sample representing those at risk suggest that O.N.C. entrants are less likely to give a high rating to their works training than the craft entrants.

TABLE 4.9

Question asked for comment on works training. Categorised in terms used by respondents

	All respondents		Interview sample			
			Totals		O.N.C. only	
	N	%	N	%	N	%
I Favourable on the whole						
1. Very good training scheme	55	12	18	14	10	11
2. Good experience but could be improved	126	>27	36	27	25	>27
3. All workmen most helpful to apprentices	29	>6	11	9	5	>5
Total	210	46	65	50	40	44
II Uncertain						
4. Would have preferred a training school or full-time instructor	26	<6	9	7	8	9
5. It was up to the individual; depended upon own initiative	52	>11	15	11	13	14
Total	78	17	24	18	21	23
III Unfavourable						
6. Lack of supervision – little interest shown by employer	71	15	17	13	13	>14
7. Time wasted – old-fashioned	19	4	7	5	3	>3
8. Cheap labour – too little training and too much emphasis on production – Firm only interested in time-keeping	81	18	18	14	14	>15
Total	171	37	42	32	30	33
Grand total	459	100	131	100	91	100

185 no response 29% of 644

35 no response 21% of 166   24 no response 21% of 115

	Interviewees	
	O.N.C.	Trade
I Favourable	40	25
II Uncertain	21	3

Chi squared with Yates's correction = 4·43 $p < 0.05$

Many respondents – over a quarter – did not add any further comments on their works training, contenting themselves with the rating scale recorded in Table 4.8. Among those who did use this second opportunity the proportion complaining is higher. It is likely that those choosing favourable ratings on the previous question were disinclined to add further eulogies. It is notoriously easier to complain than to praise.

Table 4.10 monitors job changes both before and after twenty-one and it is clear that the traditional pattern continues. About two-thirds of the O.N.C. entrants and rather more of the craft remained with the same firm for a five-year period, after which the number remaining was less than half: the O.N.C.s being the more mobile group.

TABLE 4.10

Job changes before and after reaching the age of twenty-one
(See Table A4.10, Appendix III for details)   Percentages

Samples		N	Job changes		
			Remained with same firm	Moved to other firms	Left engineering
Before 21	All respondents	644	71·3[1]	27·6[1]	1·1
	O.N.C. respondents	443	75·4[1]	23·7[1]	0·9
	All interviewees	166	63·9[3]	34·3[3]	1·8
	O.N.C. interviewees	115	66·1	32·2	1·7
After 21	All respondents	644	49·5[2]	45·2[2]	5·3
	O.N.C. respondents	443	45·8[2]	48·3[2]	5·9
	All interviewees	165	43·0[3]	53·3[3]	3·7
	O.N.C. interviewees	114	39·5	55·2	5·3

[1] Before 21: O.N.C. entrants less mobile than craft.
          Chi sq. = 11·8   p = 0·001
[2] After 21: Craft entrants less mobile than O.N.C.
          Chi sq. = 6·8   p < 0·01
[3] Among the random sample there is more movement both before and after twenty-one. Chi squared = 5·37 and 4·61 respectively (p = 0·02 and 0·05) suggesting that the more mobile young workers are under-represented among respondents. Relative differences between O.N.C. and craft entrants in the same direction as in the total samples.

The next four tables (4.11 – 4.14) relate to the jobs held by the respondents at the time of answering the questionnaire. The scale devised by Nelson used to categorise the father's job level is now applied to the sons. (See Chapter 3, Table 3.6, page 35).

TABLE 4.11

Level of job held at time of response

Level of job	O.N.C. respondents		Trade respondents		O.N.C. interviewees		Trade interviewees	
	N	%	N	%	N	%	N	%
2. Lower Professional[1]	177	40(15)[3]	17	8(8)	40	35(14)	8	16(4)
3. Highly Skilled	174	39(30)	78	39(32)	48	42(23)	19	37(34)
4. Skilled	76	17(25)	82	41(18)	23	20(26)	18	35(15)
5. Others[2]	16	4(30)	24	12(42)	4	3(37)	6	12(47)
Totals	443	100	201	100	115	100	51	100

There were marked differences between those who had started in O.N.C. classes and those initially on City and Guilds courses in the expected direction. 40 per cent of the O.N.C. respondents could be classified as professional with only 4 per cent in the two lower categories of moderately and semi-skilled workers. Among the trade students 70–80 per cent were doing skilled or highly skilled work.

The high percentage of trade interviewees in the lower professional category (16 per cent) is due to the addition of a few selected individuals to the random sample (recorded in Chapter 2, page 22). 7 per cent of trade students in this category is a more realistic figure to use for the purposes of extrapolation to all those at risk though this too is probably too high in view of the overall bias in this study in favour of 'successful' student workers.

Taking the Table 4.11 as a whole, only 40 out of the 644 respondents (about 6 per cent) were in the lower-level categories i.e.

[1] A few respondents had an associateship of one of the professional engineering institutions but the jobs they held did not clearly justify rating them in category 1. 'Higher Professional'. The one ex-trade student who was a director of a small family business is also included here in category 2. See Chapter 6, p. 94.

[2] Two-thirds of this group were in jobs rated 'Moderately Skilled'; one trade student was in a job rated 'Unskilled' and the rest were rated 'Semi-skilled'.

[3] Figures in brackets give the corresponding percentages for the level of father's job. Taken from Table 3.6, p. 35.

TABLE 4.12
Level of jobs by age: O.N.C. respondents

Level of job	1950 Sample Average age = 32·7 Percentage	1952 Sample Average age = 30·7 Percentage	1957 Sample Average age = 25·7 Percentage	1960 Sample Average age = 22·7 Percentage	Totals %	Totals N
2. Lower Professional	53	44	37	35	40	177
3. Highly Skilled	30	36	41	43	39	174
4. Skilled	13	18	17	22	17	76
5. Others	4	2	5	0	4	16
Totals	100	100	100	100	100	
N	47	85	236	79		447

below 'Skilled'. The situation is of course circular: the designation 'apprentice' implies a subsequent status at least of 'skilled worker' and in most cases includes the 'privilege' of day-release to technical college courses. Attendance at such classes in turn increases to some extent the chance of promotion within the firm. The 'O.N.C. chap' is seen by the young worker as the one who will be able to leave the bench. The total figures of course hide the sub-sample differences which are given in Table 4.12. They show a uniform and steady rise up the occupational ladder over the years with 83 per cent of sixteen-year-old starters reaching highly skilled/technician status in their early thirties. The tidy structure of Table 4.12 suggests that there was little change in the training and career patterns of engineering apprentices during the sixteen years covered by the study. Comparison of Table 4.11 with Table 3.6, p. 35 showing job level of the respondents' fathers gives some measure of social mobility among the sample of respondents. For an accurate picture it is necessary to monitor the rise or fall of each individual and this is done in Chapter 7, pp. 119–22.

Answers to the question 'How many persons, if any, do you directly control?' provided some measure of the responsibility exercised and it can be seen in Table 4.13 that three-quarters of the respondents had no direct control over the work done by other members of the firm. This figure varied with the average age of the cohort from 67 per cent for the oldest to 82 per cent for the 1960 sample.

TABLE 4.13

Question: How many persons, if any, do you directly control?

| | All respondents | | Interview sample | | | |
| | | | Totals | | O.N.C. only | |
Responses	N	%	N	%	N	%
None	488	76	125	75	94	82
1 – 4	92	14	21	13	7	6
5 – 9	17	<3	4	>2	4	>3
10 – 25	21	>3	9	<6	5	4
Over 25	13	2	5	3	3	>2
Others[1]	13	2	2	1	2	>1
Totals	644	100	166	100	115	100

[1] Includes people whose responsibility for the work of others was not continuous.

The next table (4.14) shows that about one-third of respondents (40 per cent for the O.N.C. only) worked in a drawing office at the time of response. Only 16 per cent had been recruited as apprentice draughtsmen (Table 4.4 above): others had started with a general learnership and had settled for the drawing office later. The figures fluctuate: by the time of the interview some had moved on to the sales department or were 'on the road' as technical representatives, a job described by one interviewee as 'the nearest I can get to being my own boss'. The other large group in Table 4.14 comprises those 'at the bench' in a workshop. Here, as would be expected, there are proportionately more of the City and Guilds entrants. The rest spread themselves between laboratories, retail shops, telephone exchanges and outdoor sites.

TABLE 4.14

Question: Do you work in:

	All respondents		Interview sample			
			Totals		O.N.C. only	
	N	%	N	%	N	%
A drawing office	154	26	48	30	44	40
A workshop	217	37	55	34	27	24
A laboratory	17	3	2	1	2	2
Or other – specify	204	34	57	35	38	34
Totals	590	100	162	100	111	100
	NK = 54		NK = 4		NK = 4	

Others						
(a) Supervisor's office attached to workshop	55	9	20	12	18	16
(b) Site work away from base	78	13	14	9	6	5
(c) Several places	41	7	12	>7	8	7
(d) Telephone exchange	16	3	6	<4	1	1
(e) Art studio	1	trace	1	<1	1	1
(f) Retail shop	13	2	4	>2	4	4
Sub-total	204	34	57	35	38	34

Several of the variables monitored in the preceding tables are of course interrelated. Employees of large firms account for at least half of the respondents (more among O.N.C.s and less among trade entrants). All the public bodies represented had over 1,000 employees but only 6 per cent of the contracting firms were as large as that. 41 per cent were in the smallest category. Size is related to the scale of production and to the place in which the works training is carried out. Of the 9 individuals from the smallest firms (under 100) 8 were engaged in the manufacture of 'one-offs' or prototype equipment to special order. Not surprisingly nearly 90 per cent of those engaged in mass production were in firms with over 1,000 employees.

About two-thirds of respondents were trained either in a works training school or at the bench, the former being strongly associated with large firms and the latter with small ones. Full-time instructors were of course associated with large manufacturing firms and works training schools. Detailed tables dealing with these relationships are given in Appendix III, Tables A4.14–A4.17, pp. 172–6.

Table 4.15 which relates opinions on training to size of firm indicates that satisfaction among employees of the large firms was very significantly greater than for those in the smaller ones.

TABLE 4.15

Opinion of training and size of firm

(All O.N.C. respondents 1957 and 1960 cohorts)

Column percentages

Opinion of training	I, II and III 999 and below	IV 1000+	%	N Totals
Very good	12	25	20	60
Fairly good/Moderate	60	59	59	176
Rather poor/Unsatisfactory	28	16	21	63
Totals	100	100	100	299
N	121	178	299	
Row percentages	40	60	100	

Chi squared between extreme ratings $\dfrac{15 \mid 45}{34 \mid 29} = 10\cdot8$

$p = 0\cdot001$

In the next table opinions are matched against the types of firm in which respondents worked. The public bodies are the only type of firm substantially over-represented on the 'very good' rating and the difference is significant at the 1 in 40 level. However, it is clear from Table 4.15 that the size of a firm is a dominant factor in these satisfaction ratings and 'Public Bodies' almost by definition are in the largest class whereas within each of the manufacturing 'types' apart from mass production most sizes are represented. (See Appendix III, Table A4.17, p. 176.)

During the 1960 study of 'Mackinton Tech.' Dr. Lee visited over 100 organisations representative of those whose employees attended the college and talked to the people responsible for training. The 'Public Bodies' involved included local and national government departments, a university and a college. In all such cases he found that technical college studies were 'explicitly encouraged and day

TABLE 4.16

Opinion of training and type of firm

(All O.N.C. respondents)

Column percentages

Opinion of training	Manufacturing firms[1]					Con-trac-tors	Public Bodies	Others	Grand Total	
	a	b	c	Oth's	Tot's				%	N
Very good	13	19	18	16	17	22	38	0	20	84
Fairly good and Moderate	67	54	59	68	60	57	44	100	58	250
Rather poor and Unsatisfactory	20	27	23	16	23	22	18	0	22	96
Totals	100	100	100	100	100	100	100	100	100	430
N	55	85	187	25	352	37	39	2		430
Row percentages	13	20	43	6	82	8+	9	Trace	100	

[1] a = Simple articles, few components e.g. screws
  b = Small articles, many components e.g. instruments
  c = Large articles, many components e.g. cars
Chi squared   Public Bodies/Total Manufacturing   Extreme ratings

$$\frac{15 \mid 61}{7 \mid 81} = 5\cdot31$$

$$p = 0\cdot025$$

release provision was generous'.[1] The national statistics show that administration, defence, gas, electricity and water are at the top of the batting order with approximately 100 per cent of all employees under eighteen having part-time day release.[2]

When scale of production is analysed in terms of satisfaction with the training offered, the indications are that the least satisfied employees came from firms dealing with the manufacture of 'one-offs' and prototype equipment and those on large batch production. Again, there is interaction with size, but there is an additional factor. Firms dealing with prototypes and 'one-offs' have problems, similar in some respects to those faced by contractors providing a service

TABLE 4.17

Opinion of training and scale of production

(Manufacturing industries only)

All O.N.C. respondents
Column percentages

	Scale of production					Totals	
Opinion of training	1. One-offs	2. Large batch	3. Mass pro-duction	4. Con-tinuous flow	5. Other	%	N
Very good	13	16	>21	>8	>24	17	**61**
Fairly good and Moderate	61	56	56	>83	>64	60	**211**
Rather poor and Unsatisfactory	26	28	>22	>8	11	23	**81**
Totals	100	100	100	100	100	100	353
N	**128**	**71**	**97**	**12**	**45**		353
Row percentages	36	20	>27	>3	13		100

	1 + 2	3 − 5	
Very Good	28	33	Chi sq. = 5·36
Poor and Unsatisfactory	53	27	p. = 0·02

'One-offs' and large batch production significantly associated with fewer 'Very good' ratings on training and more 'Poor and Unsatisfactory' ones.

[1] *The Young Worker at College*, ibid., p. 100.
[2] *Statistics of Education, 1970*, Vol. 3, *Further Education*, p. 60.

for individual customers. 'On the job' training and varying practical experience can be seen as more important than standardised training.[1]

In the 1950 and 1952 studies students from Building departments were included and in 1960 some Commerce and Catering students were tested and interviewed. The follow-up study was geared to engineering students only and the few others who received a questionnaire and responded were excluded from the analysis.[2] The high proportion of manufacturing industries is an inevitable consequence.

The relationship between job achievement and examination success at college is discussed in Chapter 6 but aspects of this subject – attitudes of employers to college attendance, for example – arose spontaneously during interviews or were the subject of comment on the questionnaire and these are more appropriately included here.

The following remarks were written in answer to the item in Section III of the questionnaire in which respondents were asked to look back and comment on their college careers and say whether or not they had any regrets. About 12 per cent of respondents chose to comment on their employers.[3]

'I do wish that my first company had let me continue studying.' (Failed S_1 maths first attempt and day release refused. At twenty-four in another job was allowed a day a week at college for an O.N.C. course.)

'Unfortunately I received no encouragement from my apprentice supervisor.' (College put him in an O.N.C. class and supervisor told him 'not to bother' to change to O.N.C. – wanted him to do a City and Guilds course.)

'My only regret is that the company I work for attach little importance to actual qualifications.' (Passed the second year and at age twenty-five doing third year in the evenings.)

'You are fooled into signing for an apprenticeship and it doesn't turn out the same when you get to work.'

'There were no evening classes for the course I needed, but I was twenty-one so the firm wouldn't give me day release.'

The following quotations from interview notes are deliberately

[1] For further discussion of the organisational variables see Chapter 6, pp. 104–9.
[2] See Table 2.2, p. 21.
[3] The other results on this question are dealt with in the next chapter, pp. 81–3.

overweighted with the views of those rating their training as 'Rather poor' or 'Unsatisfactory', as the favourable comments listed in Section 1 of Table 4.9 are unequivocal and require no further elaboration.

'During my first year as an apprentice I was only asked once about what I was doing at the college. When I was younger there was no-one around me who believed in education. No-one in the works had any use for theory.' At the time of the interview he was on the engineering staff of a hospital and very happy. 'All the staff are qualified or aiming to be qualified – the whole environment is conducive to study.'

'At my first firm I couldn't get on with the foreman: he wasn't trained and I could see no chance of advancement. At my second job promises had nothing to do with reality.' Now very happy in his technician's job and 'going to tech. for a hobby', taking radio amateurs' examinations 'and expecting to get a licence to transmit'.

'Any training I had was given by the electrician I happened to be working with and most of them just wanted you to do the rough work all the time.'

'There are two kinds of apprenticeship, one where you're taught properly and the other where you're just trained by an older worker. I never knew anything about sandwich courses and how to go about getting a grant.' But he is determined that his children will. 'A child has to see somebody else studying to take to it. Now that I've realised I can do it and am getting down to it my young brother has started working harder too. There's no-one else at home who studied or read books.'

The outsider sees the young worker, in the words of the Crowther Report, as 'climbing two ladders simultaneously' and the idea of a double assignment is implicit in the separation of this chapter on 'training within the firm' from the next one on technical college courses. The serious and ambitious young worker, who is almost by definition over-represented in a sample such as this one, expects the two parts of his 'apprenticeship' to be closely interlinked and most of his complaints related to the fact that these expectations were not fulfilled. The separation is an artificial one and among those who complained that their 'training' was unsatisfactory it is practically impossible to find a comment which does not incorporate some reference to the lack of integration between the two aspects.

CHAPTER 5

Serving their Time: the Technical College Ladder

The first part of Section III of the questionnaire covered at least nine topics related to the students' academic careers: which colleges they attended; courses taken; changes in courses of study; examination success by the age of twenty-one and after the age of twenty-one, followed by comments on their college experience.

Seven colleges were represented in the four initial studies on which the follow-up survey was based; four in the North-West and three in the Midlands and the students were spread over a total of twenty courses. Tables 5.1 and 5.2 show numbers and response rates by date of entry, by college and by course of study. In these and some subsequent tables response rates are based on the total number 'at risk' and are lower than the *actual* response rates given in Table 2.3, page 23 because they include the subjects who could not be traced and who did not therefore receive a questionnaire. However, the relative differences on the various vectors (e.g. individual colleges) are of some interest.

TABLE 5.1

Response rates by colleges and year of entry

The seven colleges are lettered A to G
Response rates in percentages:
Year of entry

	North-West colleges			Midland colleges		
	1950 N = 78	1952 N = 144			1957[1] N = 236	1960 N = 188
A	19·3	16·3				
B	23·0	25·9		E	42·1	
C	20·4	19·0		F	32·2	
D	25·0	26·0		G	43·1	37·6
Total	21·4	20·8		Total	39·7	37·6

[1] In the 1957 study the sample comprised O.N.C. students only.

67

TABLE 5.2

Response rates by course taken

Course taken			Year of entry				
			1950	1952	1957	1960	Totals
O.N.C. Respondents	N		47	85	236	79	447
Non-respondents	N		159	244	358	87	848
Response rates	%		23·9	25·8	39·7	47·6	34·5
Mechanical trades							
Respondents	N		19	32	—	54	105
Non-respondents	N		83	206	—	124	413
Response rates	%		18·6	13·4	—	30·3	20·3
Electrical Trades							
Respondents	N		12	27	—	55	94
Non-respondents	N		44	99	—	101	244
Response rates	%		21·4	21·4	—	35·3	27·8
Total Respondents	N		78	144	236	188	646[1]
Non-respondents	N		286	549	358	312	1505
Response rates	%		21·4	20·8	39·7	37·6	30·0

The overall figures in Table 5.1 confirm the difference in rate of response between the two older groups of subjects, whose first contact with the research worker was separated from the second by fourteen to sixteen years, and the younger ones who had a gap of only six to nine years.[2]

Table 5.2 makes clear the higher response rates from the O.N.C. students but these also decrease progressively with the remoteness of the previous contact. The overall differences shown in Table 5.1 still hold, with the 1960 trade students having a higher response rate than the earlier O.N.C. students.

For the part-time day-release student the course of study at the technical college is largely predetermined. If, as a school leaver, he takes a job which allows him a 'day off' to go to the 'tech.' he will find that his job is in most cases 'married' to a particular course of study. The implicit assumption is, not unnaturally, that his day at college will fit him to do the job better in the other four days of the week. Liberal-minded employers and educators want the experience to be rewarding for him personally – and it often is – but this is not the primary purpose. The less liberally minded make this very clear

[1] See note 2, Table 2.2, p. 21.
[2] See Chapter 2, page 21.

when and if social studies lecturers introduce controversial issues into their curricula. Such dilemmas are not the 'fault' of employers who clearly have every right to their opinions about the purpose of technical education – they are endemic in a system where 'education' takes place in the employer's time.

Tables 5.3 to 5.6 document changes in course of study and moves to other colleges. About one-third of all respondents had made a change of some kind but this figure rises to nearly half in the interview sample suggesting that those who made no change are over-represented in the respondent sample. The three respondents who had left engineering (two of whom were interviewed) merely serve to remind us of a category about whom this survey provides no significant information.

Table 5.4 deals with types of changes – from day to evening classes, O.N.C. to craft and vice versa.

Judgements about the 'level' of a course are based on academic content and continuity of study.

For example:

Same level: switching to a course on welding after completion of the three-year course in heating and ventilating.

Upward: from craft courses to O.N.C., e.g. student who did well for two years on the telecommunications course and was transferred on the advice of his training officer to the second year of O.N.C. electrical. In a few cases transfer was from O.N.C. to O.N.D. or day release to block release. 15 Trade entrants (18–3) out of a total of 201 i.e. 7·5 per cent were transferred to O.N.C. courses.

Downward: from O.N.C. to a technician or craft course: from a technician course to craft. This, as Table 5.4 shows, was the most common type of change and, since O.N.C. courses are seen as leading to better jobs, was often a source of discontent. 83 out of 443 i.e. 18·7 per cent.

Table 5.5 shows the pattern of changes over four or more years of study.

The few changes in the first year were by those who realised within a very short time that they had made the wrong choice and changed jobs, e.g. one who was 'in a factory for a month' and realised that although he 'liked playing about with mechanical things' for himself,

TABLE 5.3

Changes in course of study: nature of change

Sample			1. Left Engineering		2. Between courses in Mech. and Electrical Engineering		*Change of course* 3. Other changes		4. All course changes		5. No changes	
	N	%	N	%	N	%	N	%	N	%	N	%
Total respondents	644	100	3	0·5	36	5·6	181	28·1	220	34·2	424	65·8
O.N.C. respondents	443	100	2	0·4	32	7·2	119	26·9	153	34·5	290	65·5
Interviewees	166	100	2	1·2	13	7·8	65	39·2	80	48·2	86	51·8

TABLE 5.4

Changes in course of study: type of change

This table relates to those (numbering roughly a third in each sample) listed under Column 3 'Other changes' in Table 5.3

						Type of change							
						Remaining on day release						
			Evening classes		Same level		Upward		Downward		Mixed	
Sample	N	%	N	%	N	%	N	%	N	%	N	%
Total respondents	181	100	40	22·1	20	11·1	18	9·9	96	53·0	7	3·9
O.N.C. respondents	119	100	27	22·7	0	—	3	2·5	83	69·8	6	5·0
Interviewees	65	100	17	26·2	9	13·8	11	16·9	25	38·5	3	4·6

TABLE 5.5

Changes in course of study: year of change

This table relates to those listed under Column 4 'All course changes' in Table 5.3

Sample	N	%	Only one: Year 1st		2nd		Year of change and number of changes 3rd		4th		later		More than one	
			N	%	N	%	N	%	N	%	N	%	N	%
Total respondents	220	100	4	1·8	106	48·2	29	13·2	33	15·0	16	7·3	32	14·5
O.N.C. respondents	153	100	4	2·6	77	50·3	19	12·4	17	11·2	11	7·2	25	16·4
Interviewees	80	100	2	2·5	30	37·5	9	11·2	18	22·5	3	3·8	18	22·5

when it came 'to bending and drilling holes in 300 metal plates it was not on'. He wanted 'brain work', became a clerk and switched to a college of commerce where he found the O.N.C. in Business Studies 'very well organised'. There is obvious overlap here with those who had reported they had 'left engineering' (Table 5.3, p. 70). Approximately half the changes took place in the second year as a result of success or failure in the first year.

The final column in Table 5.5. is a mixed bag containing, for example, one who obtained an O.N.C. in Mechanical Engineering and went on without a break to do an H.N.C. in Production Engineering, and another student who registered in a General Workshop course in 1950, absented himself from the examination and was called up for National Service the following year. He went back to evening classes in 1962 alternately passing and failing, switching from one college to another and changing from General Engineering to Telecommunications and was still attempting some kind of study in 1966 at the age of thirty-three. However, he maintained that his opportunities for finding a job were 'very satisfactory' ('I always got the job I went for') and that he enjoyed his current job 'immensely'.

During the first two or three years of study less than 10 per cent of respondents changed from one college to another and most of these were to another local college. This is in line with the figure of 11 per cent quoted in *The Young Worker at College*.[1] The reasons were mainly related to a change of home address, a change of firm or convenience of travel. In the later years 22 per cent moved to colleges catering for more advanced and/or specialist work. Details are shown in Table 5.6.

TABLE 5.6
Change of college after the third year

					Changes			
			None		Other local college		More advanced or specialist college	
Sample	*Totals*							
	N	%	N	%	N	%	N	%
Total respondents	644	100	445	69	59	9	140	22
O.N.C. respondents	443	100	281	63	47	11	115	26
Interviewees	166	100	106	64	16	10	44	26

[1] Venables, 1967, p. 19.

Among the 140 who moved on to advanced study, 25 had begun in a trade course. One such student started in a General Workshop course in 1952 (after fifteen) and was transferred to an O.N.C. course the following year on the recommendation of a college teacher having obtained high scores in the tests used in the 1952 research. He was given day release until the age of twenty-three and then continued in evening classes (at a C.A.T.) and eventually became a graduate member of one of the Engineering Institutions at the age of twenty-nine. 'Damned hard work' he called it.

There was of course considerable overlap between Tables 5.5 and 5.6, since a change of course in the later years often necessitated a change of college also. Respondents made comments on the reasons for change which were in the main straightforward and obvious. 246 of the 644 respondents (i.e. 39 per cent) recorded changes of some sort and two-thirds of them gave as the reasons either that the new course was not available at the old college or that the new college was 'more convenient'. The rest indicated that the new course was either 'more appropriate' or 'easier'. (Details are given in Appendix III, Table A5.1, p. 177.)

College achievement. In the initial four studies examination success was recorded for three years in all cases and for one and two years longer in the 1960 and 1950 studies respectively. The present results record achievement after the age of twenty-one as well as providing some check on the figures for the early years of apprenticeship. The results are set out in Table 5.7.

The figures are slightly misleading in two respects. In the first place 4 per cent of the O.N.C. respondents (sixteen individuals) transferred to full-time and block-release schemes on which they achieved more success in less time and several of these subjects were deliberately included with the random sample for interview which is one reason for the higher percentages in column 4. An additional factor proved to be a bias among the respondent sample which was not detectable by means of the earlier records. These showed that those failing or absenting themselves in the early years were under-represented but those in this category who did respond proved to be overweighted with subjects who had gone on to succeed despite this early set-back.

The second point to note about this table is that just over 20 per cent of the O.N.C. starters were transferred during the first few years to trade classes. If these were excluded from the table (as they are in

74

Maximum levels achieved – percentages

Samples	N	Before and after 21	1. Less than 2.	2. O.N.C. final C. & G. 5th yr.	3. 1st yr. H.N.C.	4. H.N.C. and above
1950	78	Before	77	14	3	6
		After	59	11	4	26
1952	144	Before	73	17	8	2
		After	62	16	3	19
1957	236[1]	Before	60	26	10	4
		After	44	30	6	20
1960	188	Before	67	21	5	7
		After	62	25	5	8
Total respondents	646	Before	67	21	7	5
		After	55[2]	23	5	17
Total interviewees	166	Before	68	19	7	6
		After	57	19	4	20
O.N.C. respondents Totals	445	Before	59	25	9	7
		After	43	26	7	24
O.N.C. interviewees	115	Before	62	21	8	9
		After	47	21	6	26
Trade respondents Totals	201	Before	85	>13	<2	0
		After	80	16	1	3
Trade interviewees	51	Before	82	16	2	0
		After	78	16	0	6

[1] O.N.C. entrants only.
[2] This figure is reduced to 47 per cent if the 8 per cent of respondents who passed the (3rd year) Intermediate City and Guilds examinations are excluded.

subsequent ones) the proportions in the later column would of course be higher. 15 trade starters (7 per cent) were transferred to O.N.C. classes: 6 reached professional status and 3 of them turned up in the interview sample.

The important figures in Table 5.7 are those in columns 1 and 4. 43 per cent of O.N.C. starters and 80 per cent of those starting in trade classes had failed to reach either the Ordinary National Certificate or the Fifth Year Certificate of the City and Guilds. Indeed 55 per cent of the trade students had no success beyond the second year of a City and Guilds course. Column 4 confirms the low figure for the attainment of H.N.C. in even time (7 per cent for O.N.C. starters) which has been found in previous studies.[1] The figure of 24 per cent after further years of study indicates that those who reach the first hurdle (O.N.C.) within their first five years tend to go on trying for the higher stage even though in most cases this has to be done in evening classes.

Although the five years of study for H.N.C. or City and Guilds final are based on the supposition that these will coincide with the traditional five years' apprenticeship between 16 and 21 years of age, there were in this sample many exceptions to this rule. The mean age when these subjects were first contacted in first-year classes was 16·8 years with a range from 15+ (7 per cent, mostly in trade classes), to over 20 (4 per cent, mainly in O.N.C. classes). A majority of those who were over 16 had taken preliminary courses after leaving school and had been obliged to transfer from day-time classes to evening attendance after reaching the age of 21.

The breakdown of the results for the four sub-samples indicates in the final column of the table the steady increase in qualifications (from 8 per cent to 26 per cent) over the years after twenty-one and mirrors to some extent the rise up the occupational ladder shown in Table 4.12, p. 59. The proportions of O.N.C. students in each of the sub-samples – which clearly has an effect on the overall figures – were for 1950: 60 per cent; 1952: 59 per cent; 1957: 100 per cent; and 1960: 42 per cent (figures derived from Table 5.2, p. 68). The percentages of these O.N.C. entrants obtaining H.N.C. and beyond (column 4, Table 5.7) were, in descending order of age, 33 per cent, 56 per cent, 30 per cent and 16 per cent which combine together to give the figure of 24 per cent for the total O.N.C. respondents.

However, the most important aspect of the table is the uniformity

[1] *15 to 18*, H.M.S.O., 1959, The Crowther Report. Venables, Ethel, *The Young Worker at College*, Faber and Faber, 1967.

of the patterns of achievement between the years 1950 and 1966. Interpreting the figures optimistically and forgetting that they stem from samples biased in favour of success, one can say that at least 40 per cent of the O.N.C. entrants at risk and 70 per cent of those in City and Guilds classes abandoned college without obtaining the recognised qualification appropriate to their course of study. Many of the City and Guilds students obtained an Intermediate Certificate requiring three successful years of study but only about 20 per cent persisted beyond this to take the Fifth Year Examination.

Table 5.8 gives pass rates over four years for O.N.C. and trade respondents separately and for the combined interview samples, and shows the gradual attrition of numbers over the years.

In all the four previous studies pass rates were recorded and the constancy of pass rates in these national examinations is discussed in *The Young Worker at College*.[1] For the 1950 cohort the pass rates at the end of the first year were as follows: O.N.C. 55 per cent; City and Guilds Machine Shop and Electrical Installation 80 per cent and 66 per cent respectively;[2] combining the two trade groups, 74 per cent. Absentee rates within the first year were 9·7 per cent for the O.N.C.s and 16 per cent for the trade courses; 13·4 per cent overall. Among the respondents to the follow-up study pass rates in year one were higher and absentee rates lower, demonstrating once again the survey's bias in favour of successful and persistent students.

Column 6 of Table 5.8 gives the drop-out rates at the end of the first, second and third years. The percentages for total drop-outs (i.e. combining the O.N.C. and trade figures) are respectively 6 per cent, 16 and 30 compared with the figures for the interview sample – 7, 14 and 23 as shown.

By combining the figures for leavers after the third year (i.e. no further study recorded) with the absentees in the fourth year, the drop-outs in four years can be estimated to be 22 per cent for the O.N.C.s and 42 per cent for the Trade students (31 per cent overall in the interview sample). These are lower than the figures obtained in the 1960 study which were respectively 28 per cent, 51 per cent and 44 per cent.[3]

Table 5.9 summarises the position at the end of five years. 68 per cent of O.N.C. respondents completed the fifth year and 57 per cent persisted further. For trade respondents the comparable figures were 47 per cent and 33 per cent respectively.

After listing the courses taken and their examination results, respondents were asked: 'Can you now look back and comment on

[1] Ibid., p. 182.   [2] Ibid., p. 145.   [3] Ibid., p. 142.

Table 5.8

Success and drop out over the first four years

1. Sample	2. N	3. Sat examination		4. Pass rates	5. Absentees		6. No further study recorded	
		N	% of Col. 2	%	N	% of Col. 2	N	% of Col. 2
Year 1								
O.N.C. respondents	443	419	95	66	24	5	—	—
Trade respondents	201	186	93	77	15	7	—	—
Interviewees	166	149	90	68	17	10	—	—
Year 2								
O.N.C. respondents	443	385	87	69	34	8	24	5
Trade respondents	201	151	75	75	35	18	15	7
Interviewees	166	134	81	73	21	12	11	7

Year 3	O.N.C. respondents	**443**	**345**	78	64	**49**	11	**49**	11
	Trade respondents	**201**	**122**	61	71	**25**	12	**54**	27
	Interviewees	**166**	**116**	70	71	**26**	16	**24**	14
Year 4	O.N.C. respondents	**443**	**294**	66	69	**50**	>11	**99**	>22
	Trade respondents	**201**	**77**	38	77	**30**	15	**94**	47
	Interviewees	**166**	**99**	60	69	**28**	17	**39**	23

TABLE 5.9

Persisters after the fifth year

Sample	1. 2	No further study recorded after the fifth year								Study continuing after the fifth year					
		Sat an exam. in the fifth yr.		Pass Rates	No fifth-year examination		Total		At a technical or other college		At a Technological University		Total continuing study	
	N	N	% of Col. 2	%	N	% of Col. 2	N	% of Col. 2	N	% of Col. 2	N	% of Col. 2	N	% of Col. 2
O.N.C. respondents	443	50	11	54	139	31	189	43	233	52	21	5	254	57
Trade respondents	201	28	14	68	107	53	135	67	64	32	2	1	66	33
Interviewees	166	19	11	42	51	31	70	42	93	56	3	2	96	58

your college career. For example, do you have any regrets?' 90 per cent of respondents answered this question and their replies coded on a six-point scale are set out in Table 5.10.[1]

The following are some of the comments made:

1. *No regrets*
   'I have no regrets except that I didn't find one day a week very satisfactory.'
   'A happy eventful period of my life with no regrets.' (This student had no failures in the first five years and thus obtained an H.N.C. in the minimum time. He then took a course for the Institute of Works Managers 'which is like doing "O" levels after you've done "A" levels.')
   'No regrets. I would have liked to have known more about further courses available by the college a little earlier. Would have saved me a year.' (He started in a first-year O.N.C. class in 1957 and obtained a Dip.Tech. in 1964.)

2. *Regrets over examination failures*
   'Only regret is that I did not pass S_3 the first time.'
   'My only regret is that I failed the last year. Not that it makes much difference.'
   'Wish I had been more successful.'
   'Regret not getting O.N.C. or H.N.C.: feel that National Service and thinking about it beforehand broke my concentration and interest.'

3. *Regrets relating to college*
   'Looking back I have no regrets but feel more could have been gained by going on a block-release course.'
   'It would have been much better if I could have attended college more than one day a week.'
   'I must comment on the inability of some teachers to "put over" their subject.'
   'Yes – I wish that some teachers had made their lectures more interesting so that we could concentrate and not just take no notice.'

4. *Self-criticism*
   'Yes I do regret that I didn't try harder in the first three years instead of acting the fool and wasting time.'
   'I thought too much about having a good time.'

[1] See Chapter 4, p. 65, for those comments relating to employers.

TABLE 5.10

Comments on college careers

	Total replies	(% of total sample)	*Comments on college careers*											
			1. No regrets		2. Regrets over examination failures		3. Regrets relating to college and/or employers		4. Self-criticism		5. Felt capable of doing a more difficult course		6. Wished had taken an easier course	
Sample			N	%	N	%	N	%	N	%	N	%	N	%
All respondents	**573** 100%	(90·0)	**188**	32·8	**68**	11·9	**94**	16·4	**176**	30·7	**23**	4·0	**24**	4·2
O.N.C. respondents	**395** 100%	(89·2)	**122**	30·9	**52**	13·2	**68**	17·2	**127**	32·1	**10**	2·5	**16**	4·1
Interviewees	**152** 100%	(91·6)	**45**	29·6	**16**	10·5	**27**	17·8	**47**	30·9	**6**	4·0	**11**	7·2

'I regret not working harder but do not regret doing the course. I met many interesting people.'

'I regret my laziness after leaving school and so not taking advantage of the facilities offered.'

'I wish I had worked a bit harder at my home-work – that's what I failed most of the exams on.'

'Every time I failed I failed in only one subject – Maths. I regret not overcoming the difficulty I found with this subject.' (Passed fourth year in 1965 having started the first-year course in 1958. Had two shots at each of four examinations.)

'I wish I had continued at school instead of doing two years' National Service and three and a half years on the reserve.'

'I have no regrets on my college career – just wish I had started it at 15 instead of 18.'

'I wasn't firm enough with myself getting down to swot.'

'I have many regrets and if I had my time over again I would make sure I studied hard and not have the "come day go day" attitude I had when I was younger.'

The analysis of examination results has, so far, been done historically beginning in the first year and proceeding until no further study is recorded. In the penultimate section of this chapter we begin at the end and extract those with maximum achievement, analysing what is involved in obtaining an H.N.C. by the part-time route, by taking a close look at the pattern of pass and failure over the years. To obtain an accurate assessment of how long the part-time O.N.C. students were prepared to persist in their pursuit of a qualification it is necessary to modify Table 5.7 by excluding respondents who had either transferred to trade courses or to O.N.C. block-release, which has been done in Table 5.11. This table gives the overall figures for the 447 O.N.C. respondents and the 115 O.N.C. interviewees.

In Table 5.12 the levels of success of the O.N.C. interviewees in the preceding table are broken down according to year of entry. The different success rates after the fifth year reflect the length of time available to retake the examinations and the totals column, as in Table 5.7, can be seen to hide more than it reveals. Because of the bias in favour of those who passed the final examinations, even among those who failed in the early years, the success rates must be regarded as over-estimates and we must await the results of the National Survey for more reliable figures.

TABLE 5.11

Levels of success: O.N.C. entrants and interviewees only

Levels of success	Total O.N.C. respondents				O.N.C. interview sample			
	a) By the age of 21		b) By 1966		a) By the age of 21		b) By 1966	
	N	%	N	%	N	%	N	%
H.N.C. ± Professional Qualifications	24	5 +	94	22	7	7	28	26
O.N.C. + first-year H.N.C.	113	26	114	26	29	26	21	19
Transfer to City & Guilds No success O.N.C. years 1 and 2	294	68+	223	52	73	67	60	55
Total taking a part-time course	431	100	431	100	109	100	109	100
Number transferred to full-time and block-release courses	16 = 4% of 447				6 = 5% of 115			

TABLE 5.12

Levels of success: four cohorts of O.N.C. students by year of entry

Randomised sample: percentages

(a) = By the age of 21
(b) = By 1966

Levels of success	1950		1952		1957		1960		Totals	
	(a)	(b)	(a)	(b)	(a)	(b)	(a)	(b)	(a)	(b)
H.N.C. ± professional qualifications	8	42	9	43	4	22	9	9	7	26
O.N.C. + first-year H.N.C.	8	3	28	14	31	17	23	41	26	19
Transfers to City and Guilds No success O.N.C. years 1 and 2	84	50	63	43	65	61	68	50	67	55
Total taking a part-time course	100% 12		100% 21		100% 54		100% 22		100% 109	
Number transferred to full-time and block-release courses	0		1 = 4% of 22		2 = 4% of 56		3 = 12% of 25		6 = 5% of 115	
Mean age in 1966	32·8 years		30·7 years		25·8 years		22·6 years			

Samples by year of entry

TABLE 5.13

Proportions improving their qualifications after the age of twenty-one   O.N.C. entrants   *Percentages*

Level of improvement achieved after the age of twenty-one	Cohorts: by year of entry and number of years at risk[1]			
	1950: 11 years	1952: 9 years	1957: 6 years	1960: 1 year
H.N.C. + professional qualifications	13 + 24 = 37	16 + 13 = 29	9 + 7 = 16	0 + (1+) = 1+
O.N.C. + first-year H.N.C.	(6+)+(6+)=13	6 + 5 = 11	9 + 3 = 12	10 + (1+) = 11+
Qualifications improved	50% in 11 years	40% in 9 years	28% in 6 years	13% in 1 year
Minor changes: below O.N.C.	2	8	3	0
City & Guilds transfers	11	7	27	29
No changes	37	45	42	58
Total taking part-time courses	100% = 46	100% = 84	100% = 232	100% = 69
Transferred to full-time and block-release courses	1 = 2% of 47	1 = 1% of 85	5 = 2% of 237	9 = 12% of 78

[1] Number of years at risk = 1966 minus (year of entry plus five).

In Table 5.13 we look in detail at the changes in attainment after the fifth year. Comparison between Table 5.13 and the previous two is not possible because the 'no changes' item includes those who obtained the Ordinary or the Higher National Certificate within the five-year period.

In the next two tables we look at the patterns of pass and failure over the years and estimate the average number of years taken to qualify after leaving school. Table 5.14 presents the pattern of progression followed by fifteen O.N.C. starters and two trade starters who later transferred to the National Certificate route. They were chosen to represent the two extremes in each cohort – the quickest travellers and the slowest – and to show two or three in an intermediate position. For the 1960 group only two were available (in the random sample) but since only six years had elapsed since they had registered for the course very little variation of pattern was possible. In their case a study of the progression of those who attained O.N.C. in the six years is more relevant. There were nine of them in the random sample and the average time taken to succeed in the three years of the course after leaving school was 4·9 years with a range of 3–8. The average age was 20·9 ranging from 19 to 23.

The 1950 cohort, and to a lesser extent the one starting in 1952, were involved in compulsory national Service though students doing well on recognised courses were generally able to postpone their service until they qualified. Practice varied as did their later reactions to the choices they had made. Some felt that the experience of life in one of H.M. Forces was invaluable and had helped them to appreciate the worth of 'education'. Others, predictably, saw it as a useless interruption. In Table 5.15 the average times taken to reach an H.N.C. are shown. Years spent in the Forces have been deducted for the sake of comparability with regard to time, but other effects of the experience are not so easily measured. The achievements of an ex-service family man studying three nights a week are only superficially comparable with those of a bachelor of twenty or so working for a firm allowing him to study in the day-time.

It is fairly clear from the last two tables that defining the part-time system as the 'long haul' or 'qualifying the hard way' does not overstate the case. Indeed, knowing the approximate failure rates per year, a simple model of the operation of the system can be devised to cover a five-year period of examinations.

The one set out in Figure 1 rests on three assumptions viz., that pass rates are uniform at 65 per cent throughout the system, that no

TABLE 5.14

Seventeen samples of individual progress to H.N.C. through the part-time system

	1950	1951	1952	1953	1954	1955	1956	1957	1958	1959	1960	1961	1962	1963	1964	1965	1966	Date of birth	Age of leaving school	Type of school attended
O.N.C. Entrants 1950	1	F	2	NS	NS	X	X	X	X	X	X	X	Rd	3	F	4	5	1932	17	G
	A	NS	NS	X	X	Rd	X	X	Rd	1	2	3	4	5	5+	5+	PQ	1933	15	G
	A	A	NS	NS	3	Rd	F	2	3	A	4	5						1933	16+	G
										5+	5+	5+	PQ					1935	15	T
Trade Entrant	T_1	F	T_2	T_3	X	X	X	X	Rd	1	2	3	4	5	5+	5+	PQ	1934	16	G
O.N.C. 1952 Entrants		A	1	X	X	F	NS	NS	Rd	F	2	Rd	F	3	F	4	5	1936	16	T
		A	2	3	F	4	4	X	X	X	4	5	5	5+	5+	5+	Cg	1936	16	G
		F	1	2	F	3	5	5+	NS	Rd	Ad	Ad	5	5+	5+			1935	15	M
Trade Entrant		T_1	T_2	T_3	NS	NS	NS	NS	Rd	1	2	3	X	4	5	5+	PQ	1936	15	T
													Ad					1934	15	M
O.N.C. 1957 Entrants								P	F	T_1	1	2	3	4	5	5	Cg	1937	15	M
								P	1	2	3	3	4	5	5+	5+	PQ	1940	15	T
								P	1	F	3	4	4	5	5+	5+	PQ	1940	15+	M
								P	1	2	4	4+	4+	5	5+	5+	PQ	1941	16	M
								F	F Tr	T_2	T_3	T_4	T_5	2	3	4	5	1940	15	M
1960 O.N.C. Entrants											X	1	2	3	4	5	Cg	1944	16+	Comp
											X	1	2	3	4	5	Cg	1943	16	M

Key

1–5 Passes at each of the 5 stages to H.N.C.	A Absent examination after attending classes
T_1–T_5 Passes at each of the 5 stages on a trade course	Ad Additional Study
5+ Endorsements towards H.N.C.	Cg Study continuing
4+ Endorsements taken between first and second years finals	F Failure

G Secondary Grammar School
M Secondary Modern School
NS National Service
P Preliminary courses
PQ Professional qualifications

Rd Re-registered after absence
T Secondary Technical School
Tr Transferred
X No attendance

TABLE 5.15

From School to H.N.C.   **Randomised sample**

(a) **Average time between leaving school and qualifying**
(b) **Average number of years at technical college before qualifying**
(c) **Average age when certificate obtained**

	Cohorts								
	1950		1952		1957		1960		Totals
	N = 12		N = 21		N = 54		N = 22		N = 109
	N	%	N	%	N	%	N	%	N	%
Numbers reaching H.N.C. and above	5	42	9	43	12	22	2	9	28	26
(a)	9·6[1]		8·7[1]		7·2		5·5			
Range	6–12 yrs		6–12 yrs		6–9 yrs		5–6 yrs			
(b)	8·6[1]		8·0[1]		6·3		5·0			
Range	6–12 yrs		5–12 yrs		6–7 yrs		Both 5			
(c)	28·0		25·0		22·5		21·5			
	(— 1·6)		(— 0·9)							
Range	21–30		21–34		21–24		21–22			

student drops out before experiencing four failures and that drop out after four failures is total. The reality is that students drop out at all stages of the course and would rarely be allowed to continue either on day release or on the National Certificate course after four failures. Thus the likelihood of as many as 39 per cent of any cohort (i.e. 21 + 18 in final column) achieving an H.N.C. in the seventh or eighth years after entry is remote.

Education Statistics for the United Kingdom 1970 (H.M.S.O. 1972) reports the numbers entering and succeeding in final H.N.C. examinations. The percentages passing in Mechanical Engineering increased from 59 per cent in 1966 to 67 per cent in 1968. In 1969 it fell to 65·8 per cent of a much reduced number of entrants and in 1970 there were only 23 entrants of whom 8 passed. The Engineering course had grown in numbers and had a pass rate of nearly 79 per cent in 1969 and of 75 per cent in 1970. 'All entrants' included in these tables comprise of course students with varying entry standards and those studying on block-release schemes, so that an allowance of 65 per cent overall is a realistic – perhaps an optimistic – estimate.

[1] Years on National Service not included. These averaged 1·6 for the 1950 cohort and 0·9 for 1952.

Figure 1

Model of the H.N.C. examination system

Assuming (1) Uniform pass rates of 65 per cent
(2) Drop out after the fourth failure

Pattern of success, failure and drop out

H.N. Certificate obtained with:

H.N.C. 71%

	No Success 1 Pass	2 Passes	3 Passes	4 Passes	5 Passes	No Failure	1 Failure	2 Failures	3 Failures	
		Year 1	Year 2	Year 3	Year 4	Year 5	Year 6	Year 7	Year 8	

Enter — 100 — 65 — 42 — 27 — 18 — 12 — 12

65 → 23 → 15 → 9 → 6 → 12

1 Failure: 35 — 46 — 45 — 38 — 31 — 20

23 → 30 → 29 → 25 → 20

46 → 16 → 16 → 13 → 11 → 20

2 Failures: 12 — 24 — 32 — 34 — 33 — 21

8 → 16 → 21 → 22 → 21

24 → 8 → 11 → 12 → 12 → 12 → 21

3 Failures: 4 — 11 — 18 — 24 — 28 — 18

3 → 7 → 12 → 16 → 16 → 18

4 — 1 — 4 — 6 — 8 — 10 — 18

4th Failure: drop out 29%

The overall figure of 7 per cent achieving an H.N.C. in five years (Tables 5.11 and 5.12) bears comparison with the model as do the increasing proportions qualifying over time set out in Table 5.13.

The in-built failure rate on these courses has been there for all to see for many years but the use of a standard cut-off is not admitted. It has been said that it is a device to limit the number of 'qualified' engineers: it is certainly seen as something of a gamble by the victims.

CHAPTER 6

Technical College Achievement and Level of Job

The two preceding chapters have dealt respectively with occupational level and success in college examinations. In this one the interaction between these two variables is examined.

The patterns for O.N.C. entrants and Trade entrants are set out in Table 6.1 using the randomised samples. The four totals columns mirror the information given for these interviewees in Table 4.11, p. 58, and 5.7, p. 75, and they are comparable with the figures for all other samples. A more detailed breakdown of the results is given in the Appendix III, Table A6.1, p. 178/9.

Among the respondents to this enquiry $35 + 42 = 77$ per cent of those registering in O.N.C. courses had jobs in categories 2 or 3 after a period varying from six to sixteen years. 26 per cent had achieved an H.N.C. and a further 27 per cent an O.N.C. The rest had had little or no academic success. 18 in 26 i.e. about 7 in every 10 of those with an H.N.C. had achieved marginally professional status but almost half of those in such jobs did not have a higher certificate ($\frac{16}{35}$). Indeed a fifth ($\frac{7}{35}$) were in the lowest college achievement group. It is therefore not surprising that those I interviewed who had struggled along this route had a very clear perception that it was a gamble. They didn't need the figures: these only serve to confirm what most of them already knew from experience. Most of those with no success at college amd in engineering jobs rated category 2 pre-empted questioning by 'confessing' that they had been 'lucky'. In two cases their 'luck' had prompted them to go back to 'school'. One who said he had had 'an unusual' stroke of luck claimed to be self-taught. He had 'read the books night after night' until he had 'mastered' them. Others were directors or managers of small businesses which included a butcher's shop, a furniture shop and electrical retailing.

As can be seen from the table, 37 per cent ($21 + 16$) of the O.N.C. starters were skilled tradesmen with little college success to their credit.

TABLE 6.1

Job level and technical college achievement after the age of twenty-one

Interview samples   *Overall percentages*

		College achievement										
		O.N.C. interviewees N = 115					Trade interviewees N = 51					
Job level	Examples	1. Less than 2.	2. O.N.C. final (C. & G. year 5)	3. O.N.C. H.N.C. year 1	4. H.N.C. final and beyond	Totals	1. Less than 2.	2. C. & G. year 5 (O.N.C. final)	3. C. & G. H.N.C. year 1	4. H.N.C. final and beyond	Totals
2. Lower Professional	Engineering Draughtsman and Designer. Scientific Technician. Director of small business.	7	6	>3	>18	35	8	2	nil	6	16
3. Highly Skilled	Toolmaker Electrical Fitter Foreman. Draughtsman	21	>11	>3	7	42	27	10	nil	nil	37
4. Skilled	Fitter. Turner. Senior Storeman	>16	<3	nil	<1	20	31	4	nil	nil	35
5/6. Moderately and Semi-Skilled	Sheet Metal Workers Plumbers. The more skilled factory operatives	>2	<1	nil	nil	3	12	nil	nil	nil	12
Totals		47	21	6	26	100	78	16	0	6	100

Some had transferred to City and Guilds courses and had some regrets that they had not started there. 3 per cent ranked only as moderately skilled workers: these were not, as one might expect, people of low ability who had registered on the wrong course. None of those interviewed fell into that category – test scores were at or above the norm and in most cases good school records had led to the choice of a National Certificate course rather than a City and Guilds. There is no stereotype – each was an individual story – though in most cases there had been strongly expressed preferences for practical work on leaving school.

Jack Painter was one such who had 'passed for the technical school' and left at fifteen with a good record. In his answers to the questionnaire he had nothing but praise for the attitude of his schoolmasters and the help he had been given. It was his own attitude which he regretted. 'I got a fair deal and failed because I didn't show enough interest.' Of his son's education he wrote: 'If any son of mine gets a fair crack of the whip like I did, he will have nothing to grumble about and only himself to blame if he doesn't do better than I did.' By the time of the interview he had found a new job with a firm which had decided to 'do away with piece work' and pay a basic rate to their tradesmen. He and his wife thought they would much prefer this – 'can plan your money better' – so they were going to give it a year's trial.

The pattern of employment for the City and Guilds entrants is not as different as might be expected from that of the O.N.C. apprentice. Reference has already been made to the 6 per cent who transferred to the O.N.C. stream and achieved maximum success, but in addition a further 10 per cent (a fifth of whom had the full City and Guilds Certificate) had jobs in the lower professional category. Two of these were in partnership with their fathers and two with their fathers-in-law. Another had become an assistant lecturer teaching craft students and he had just returned to (another) college in the hope of completing the City and Guilds course he had abandoned eight years earlier.

Of the rest, 72 per cent were skilled or very skilled workers and only 14 per cent were certificated. Skilled status usually follows the completion of an apprenticeship and very few saw any value in obtaining a City and Guilds Certificate. Most of those who had achieved it had in fact been promoted from the bench.[1]

[1] Confirming Cotgrove's finding in 'Education and Occupation', *Brit. J. Sociol.*, Vol. 13, No. 1, 1962, p. 39.

Of the 12 per cent who were doing labouring or semi-skilled work, most were content. Some were doing piece work because the pay was attractive; another did a job in order to keep body and soul together but spent all his spare time preaching and working with the Four Square Gospellers. He said he would be willing to support his child to go to a university although the thing he had against universities was that they are 'atheistic'. 'We don't believe in evolution so a son of mine would only be ridiculed there.' His apprenticeship had been interrupted by the war. He wasn't allowed deferment at eighteen because of his conscientious objection and so 'went to prison for four months. Interesting experience to be treated as a criminal – quite enlightening. The Army is said to broaden your outlook: prison does it too.' He was satisfied with his job 'in view of my beliefs – this form of society will soon be coming to an end.'

One comment which is typical of a general attitude among trade students was: 'The only qualification you need is a bit of know-how and a union card. You can pick most of it up at work.' One young man had passed the first year of an O.N.C. course and failed the second year. Day release then ceased and he tried evening attendance but 'couldn't keep up with it'. It was clear in the interview, however, that he felt himself to be a success. 'My standard of education is a bit higher than those I work with: I can read drawings and things like that better than they can.' He was 'very content with bench work' and didn't want 'management'. 'Me father's the same – more satisfaction in doing the job.'

A fairly typical attitude was expressed by a maintenance man in an electrical engineering works. 'The tech. gives you too much theory for my type of job: the Electrical Engineer, now he's the theory bloke but we chaps have to put him right.' 'Mind you,' he went on, 'I might just have been lucky here – having a good mate who taught me properly.' 'People are too much attached to letters behind yer name. The practical man isn't properly appreciated – yer either 'ave it in yer head or yer hands.' He had very low test scores but the only reference he made to his difficulties as a student was that classes were too large. 'Yer get lost in the swim really.' He was very much in charge of himself and highly self-respecting. His family had always lived in rented premises so 'I feel I've done all right – I can't grumble. Own me own car and am buying my house.' He evinced an air of kindly tolerance towards people like myself and the college staff.

Nelson's classification of job levels used in this study[1] is a broad

---

[1] Shown in full in Appendix II.

one using only a seven-point scale and a few of the people categorised at level 2 could be considered to be border-line cases. Among these engineers there was a very wide variety of job titles and the distinction between a 'scientific technician' (category 2) and a highly skilled technician 'with special training and a fair amount of responsibility' (category 3) is a fine one. None of the respondents was in a job at the top level – professional – although some had passed the so-called 'professional examinations' after obtaining an H.N.C. It is not surprising therefore that many of those who had succeeded at the college were discontented with their industrial status. The table provides some justification for the oft-repeated sentiment, expressed in a variety of ways, that employers take little notice of technical college examinations. In Section III of the questionnaire dealing with technical college education, this problem was examined by means of seven additional questions, some aimed at those who had obtained a certificate and others at those who had failed to do so. Responses are set out in Tables 6.2 to 6.8.

The first two are concerned with those subjects who left before obtaining a recognised certificate but not everyone in this category replied.

TABLE 6.2

Question: Reasons for discontinuing study: addressed to those who left college before obtaining a certificate

	N	% of those replying	% of total sample
1. National Service	**30**	18	5
2. Firm's decision, usually because of examination failure	**48**	28	>7
3. Student's decision Lack of interest specifically stated	**54**	31	>8
Other reasons including 'too much travelling', 'making no progress', 'further study of no value on the job'	**40**	23	6
Total replying	**172**	100	27
No reply	**472**		73
Total sample	**644**		100

These replies bore no relation to the nature of the respondent's jobs: they were randomly distributed between the levels.

96

TABLE 6.3

Question: Though you failed to obtain a certificate do you feel your studies were of some value to you? Add comments

	N	% of those replying	% of total sample
1. Some help on the job	65	62	10
2. Some personal satisfaction	24	23	4
3. Of no value	16	15	2
Total replying	105	100	16
No reply	539		84
Total sample	644		100

Tables 6.4 to 6.8 which follow are also self-explanatory.

TABLE 6.4

Question: Were your studies recognised in any way by your firm e.g. bonus, increase in wages, promotion? Give details and add comments

Sample	N	%	No recognition N	%	Bonus or gift N	%	Increased wages N	%	Bonus and wage increase N	%	Promot'n or improved training facilities N	%
O.N.C. respondents NK[1] = 124 − 28% of 443	319	100	163	51	58	18	62	>19	11	>3	25	8
Trade respondents NK = 72 = 36% of 201	129	100	76	59	20	15	15	12	3	2	15	12
O.N.C. interviewees NK = 40 = 35% of 115	75	100	31	>41	16	>21	16	>21	3	4	9	12
Trade interviewees NK = 18 = 35% of 51	33	100	19	58	5	15	3	9	2	6	4	12

	O.N.C.	Trade	
No recognition	163	76	
Some	156	53	Chi squared = 2·26 p > 0·1

[1] NK = not known.

169 people (about 26 per cent) added comments.
1. Favourable   N = 53 = 8 per cent
 Examples:
'The bonus is a good incentive.'
'Increase for those gaining an O.N.C. or similar certificate greater than for other employees.'
'We are allowed to continue at college on full pay after apprenticeship is complete.'
These replies bore no relation to the nature of the respondent's jobs: they were randomly distributed between the levels.

2. Neutral   N = 27 = 4 per cent
 Examples:
'Promotion is according to age not qualifications.'
'We get no increase but firm is appreciative and reasonable over sickness absence.'
'Promotion is on ability only.'

3. Critical   N = 89 = 14 per cent
 Examples:
'The value of technical qualifications is not appreciated by my employer '
'We get an increase only when apprenticeship is complete.'
'Not sufficient use is made by the employer of the abilities of the employee.'

One of the youngest respondents who had been an indentured apprentice in the motor industry and had had a very successful technical college career including an Associateship of one of the Colleges of (Advanced) Technology (A.C.T.) wrote:

'My firm does NOT recognise qualifications AT ALL i.e. no bonus, no wage increase, no promotion. I would like to know of a firm that does.'
Mr. A. aged 25, 8 years at Tech. and A.C.T.
Mr. B. aged 25, nothing, nothing both the same wage.'

This man was convinced that only the 'degree man' had any chance and when asked in the interview about his son's education, he replied 'University – definitely.'
16 per cent of the sample reported that it was a condition of their present employment that they should hold a particular technical certificate (Table 6.5) but on the next question, whether they themselves considered their qualification was essential, only 12 per cent

replied in the affirmative though a further 21 per cent regarded it as desirable (Table 6.6).

TABLE 6.5

Question: Is it a condition of your present appointment that you must have attained a particular technical qualification?

	N	% of those replying	% of total sample
1. A qualification is not essential	201	48	31
2. A qualification is essential	103	25	16
3. A qualification is desirable	62	15	10
4. Said to be needed for promotion, but a qualification does not guarantee promotion	29	7	>4
5. Ability to do the job is the criterion, not a paper qualification	18	4	3
6. Miscellaneous replies:	4	1	>1

Examples: Must hold a union card
    Good character the important thing
    Must have served an apprenticeship			

Total replying	417	100	65
No reply	227		35
Total sample	644		100

One reply under coding 4 ran 'Not needed for promotion if you stay with the same firm, only if you want to move.'

TABLE 6.6

Question: Do you consider the qualification you now hold is

	N	% of those replying	% of total sample
1. Essential	80	18	12
2. Desirable	134	31	21
3. Of some value	132	30	21
4. Irrelevant	89	21	14
for your present position?			
Total replying	435	100	68
No reply	209		32
Total sample	644		100

Ratings of the usefulness of college-taught subjects are set out in Table 6.7 and 238 (37 per cent) added comments.

TABLE 6.7

Question: How far have you used the knowledge gained at college in your industrial job? Ratings were set out on a four-point scale from 'Regularly' to 'Never'

1. Science and Mathematics:	All but 75 respondents (8·5%) reported some use of these subjects. Over 500 (78%) reported constant use of one or both: for the rest use was 'occasional' or 'rare'.
2. Workshop practice:	79 respondents (12%) reported no use and over two-thirds (427) reported regular use. The rest rated their use of workshop practice as 'occasional' or 'rare'.
3. Other subjects:	In addition to the need for the three basic subjects listed in 1. and 2. above, 309 respondents (48%) listed 'other' subjects which they needed on the job. Subjects mentioned were (naturally) those listed in most technical college prospectuses: electronics, strength of materials, technical drawing, thermodynamics, metallurgy and so on. A few included more specialist topics and there was some mention of English and management studies.

1. Course not of great practical use: only elementary knowledge needed.   N = 104 = 16 per cent
   Examples:
   'Most calculations and formulae can be easily looked up in tables without requiring you to calculate them.'
   'The level of maths [other subjects also mentioned] is too high for the ordinary job.'
   'Although used regularly, usually not at the depth taught at school.'
   'Simple calculations only.'
   'Design of machine tools still relys [sic] to a large extent on practical experience.'
   'Problems which require technical knowledge are just about non-existent.'
   'What knowledge I use I learned at school not at college.'
   'I don't mean to suggest that college was a waste of time, it's just that most things seem to have to be done different at work.'

2. Quite useful on the job   N = 92 = 14 per cent
   Examples:
   'Maths and Science and Workshop Practice all apply to plumbing.'

'These four subjects are essential to my trade.' (Electrician)
'My knowledge gained at college is of valuable assistance for special jobs.'
'Wouldn't say technical college was *absolutely* essential – common sense obtained from public school I use regularly.'
'I use workshop practice all the time and maths, mainly trigonometry, now and again.'

3. Miscellaneous comments   N = 45 = 7 per cent
   Examples:
   'Social studies irrelevant – should be omitted.'
   'Studies could have been more relevant.'
   'Instructors lack practical experience.'
   'My college education has given me an appreciation of the subjects and knowledge of where to look for information.'
   'My studies increased my knowledge generally and gave me a broader outlook.'
   'Working at the tech gave me confidence.'

4. No comment   N = 406 = 63 per cent

TABLE 6.8

Question: Looking back do you think the years of study were worth while? a) for the job you do and b) for personal satisfaction. Each section a) and b) was rated on a five-point scale from 'Yes, definitely' to 'Definitely not'. Space was provided for comment

	a) Value of study for the job N	%	b) for personal satisfaction N	%
1. Yes, definitely	210	33	327	51
2. Yes, on the whole	234	36	185	29
3. Uncertain	61	9	41	6
4. No, on the whole	72	11	33	5
5. Definitely not	37	6	25	4
6. No answer	30	5	33	5
Totals	644	100	644	100

Comments on each section were collated into eight groups.

a) *Value of study for the job*	N	%
1. No value – all learning done on the job	31	5
2. Able to use tools and understand job	129	20

101

3. All education and experience is worthwhile 70 11
4. Certificates help personal ambition 36 5
5. Job impossible without training 64 10
6. Have knowledge in hand in case of job
change and/or promotion 62 10
7. Gives confidence 67 11
8. Develops thinking capacity 42 7
No comment 143 22

644 100

b) *Value of study for personal satisfaction* N %
1. At the time, day at college seemed wasted 15 2
2. Course irrelevant 43 < 7
3. Valueless – as good or better position
without study 29 < 5

Sub-total 87 < 14

4. Knowing one is doing the job correctly 36 > 5
5. Sense of achievement 95 15
6. Demonstrates that the student has
intelligence 17 > 2
7. Recognition by employers 7 1
8. Valuable both theoretically and socially 69 11

Sub-total 224 > 34

No comment 333 < 52

Grand total 644 100

The picture presented so far in Tables 6.1 to 6.8 indicates that
the main determinant of job level is the fact of having spent the early
years of employment in a traineeship of some kind. If, on top of this,
a technical certificate has been gained the chances of promotion to
technician status are considerably increased. Nevertheless promotion
is by no means restricted to the certificate holder as is clear from
Table 6.1, p. 93.

The experience of technical education, whether successfully completed or not, is valued for itself – it is a help on the job and knowing a few more answers than the next man is personally satisfying. Recognition of successful study by employers is chancy. About a third of the sample did not reply to the question and among the rest about half reported some recognition in the form of bonuses, increased wages, promotion or better training facilities.

Only 103 out of 644 (16 per cent) were in jobs for which a technical qualification is a requirement and about 20 of them did not themselves regard it as really essential. 89 (14 per cent) thought the qualification they held was 'irrelevant'. This did not mean that they regarded all the knowledge acquired at college as irrelevant, simply that the examination syllabus was more advanced than was needed. Comments included mention of a sense of achievement which was valuable socially and it was clear that for many attendance at college had given them an enhanced sense of personal worth.

Among those who were successful at college, one source of frustration is that a certificate does not guarantee promotion, and another is that the H.N.C. might get you so far but not far enough. Personality factors as well as competence clearly have a bearing on promotion and in a few cases (one of which seemed to be very serious) personal difficulties were obvious during the interview; lack of interpersonal skills, poor appearance and speech were likely explanations in others. As perceived by the respondents, the differences were largely due to differences in policy and practice between firms. Some saw their employers as playing fair – 'it was up to me to get the certificate and then I was O.K.' Others were sure that it 'is the colour of your eyes that matters'. Whatever the reality, it was obvious that many employees were far from clear about the promotion policies of their employers.

The interaction between college achievement and job level was the main focus of this retrospective study which, by its very nature, could not provide reliable information about the actual situation at the working face. However, questions were included on the questionnaire related to two aspects of the organisation in which the respondent had done his early training i.e. 'served his apprenticeship'. As we have seen in Chapter 4 (Table 4.10) 50·5 per cent of them had moved to other organisations at the time of response but reference to the records of the earlier studies was reassuring: those who had felt able to reply to these questions can be regarded as reliable reporters.

Information on a third variable – the size of the firm – was available on the cards for about two-thirds of the sample, but before dealing with the analysis of these items some introductory notes on relevant sociological studies are necessary for the benefit of the general reader.

Veblen was probably the first social scientist to speculate about the psychology and sociology of work[1] and as a result of empirical studies carried out during the past fifty years or so there is now a considerable body of literature on the relationships between types or systems of production in technological industries and the attitudes and behaviour of employees. A. K. Rice used the term 'socio-technical system' to indicate that a production system requires both a technological organisation and a work organisation of those who carry out the tasks. 'The technological demands place limits on the type of work organisation possible, but a work organisation has social and psychological properties of its own that are independent of technology.'[2]

Other organisation theorists who have made notable contributions in this field are (the late) Joan Woodward[3] and her team of co-workers at Imperial College and John Goldthorpe[4] of Nuffield College, Oxford. Professor Woodward broke away from the broad general categories used by Weber and his successors (on, for example, systems of authority) and investigated the relationships between more specific features within the firms she studied, such as size, type (e.g. manufacturing or contracting), the nature of the product and the techniques of production. Hers was one of the first attempts to make a systematic classification of technology for the purpose of sociological analysis. She postulated that the type and complexity of the products a firm makes, determine the technology to be used and

[1] See, for example, Veblen, Thorstein, *The Theory of Business Enterprise*, Charles Scribner's Sons, 1904; and *The Instinct for Workmanship*, Norton & Co., N.Y., 1914.

[2] Rice, A. K., *Productivity and Social Organisation*, Tavistock Publications, 1958, p. 4. See also Emery, F. E. and Trist, E. L., 'Socio-Technical Systems' in Churchman, C. W. and Verhulst, M. (Eds.), *Management Science: Models and Techniques*, Vol. 2, Pergamon Press, Oxford, 1960, pp. 83–97.

[3] See, for example, (a) Woodward, Joan, *Management and Technology*, H.M.S.O., London, 1958. (b) Woodward, Joan, *Industrial Organisation: Theory and Practice*, O.U.P., 1965. (c) Woodward, Joan (Ed.), *Industrial Organisation: Behaviour and Control*, O.U.P., 1970. (d) Wedderburn, Dorothy and Crompton, Rosemary, *Workers' Attitudes and Technology*, C.U.P., 1972.

[4] Goldthorpe, John H., Lockwood, David, Bechhofer, Frank and Platt, Jennifer – a three-volume study of 'The Affluent Worker', C.U.P. Vol. 1 *Industrial Attitudes and Behaviour*, 1968. Vol. 2 *Political Attitudes and Behaviour* 1968. Vol. 3 (*The Affluent Worker*) *in the Class Structure*, 1969.

devised an eleven-point scale of production systems[1] within manu-facturing industry from unit and small batch production to large batch and mass production followed by varieties of process produc-tion.

To summarise some of her findings: in unit production there has to be co-ordination of functions and centralised authority; mass pro-duction, on the contrary, demands extensive specialisation and delegation of authority. In process industries the production plant 'controls' the employees. In contracting work the emphasis is on practical work and 'on the job' training and the individual worker (e.g. builder, electrician) is likely to identify with his trade union rather than with the employing firm. Such differences imply differ-ences in social groupings at the working face. For example in her report of her early work at South East Essex Technical College, she wrote that factors related to process production such as smaller working groups, the increased ratio of supervisors to operators 'were conducive to industrial peace' whereas 'these problems were much more difficult for firms using the middle ranges [i.e. batch production] than those in unit or process production'.[2]

Goldthorpe and his fellow workers in their study of 'The Affluent Worker' chose their sample from three firms with widely differing production systems on the lines of the Woodward investigation, but they were at the same time critical of her approach 'for two clearly related reasons: first because of its neglect of the way in which workers' own definitions of the work situation (their work roles included) may significantly determine their attitudes and behaviour in this situation, to some extent independently of its "objective" features; and secondly because of the limitation which is implied in seeking to explain industrial attitudes and behaviour entirely from the point of view of the functioning of the enterprise and thus ignoring the possibility of explanation from the point of view of the actors themselves, considered not only as workers but also in their various other social roles as members of families, communities, social classes and so on'.[3]

A main aim of their study was to test empirically the widely accepted thesis of working class *embourgeoisement*: the thesis that, as manual workers and their families achieve relatively high incomes and living standards, they assume a way of life which is more

[1] Woodward, Joan, *Industrial Organisation: Theory and Practice*, ibid., p. 39.
[2] Woodward, Joan, *Management and Technology*, ibid., p. 18.
[3] Vol. 1, ibid., p. 45.

characteristically 'middle class' and become in fact progressively assimilated into middle-class society.[1] The findings on this topic are discussed in the next chapter but it must be mentioned here since this particular aim dictated the choice of their sample. It consisted of 229 male employees working in shop-floor jobs, aged between twenty-one and forty-six, married and living with their wives in or near Luton. Both the men and their wives were interviewed so that data on family and social life could be included. In addition for comparative purposes a sample of 54 'low level (non-managerial) white collar employees' was drawn from the same three firms which provided the shop-floor sample. In their conclusions they state that among the semi-skilled men 'no attitudinal or behavioural patterns are in evidence that can be systematically related to the contrasting technological environments in which these men perform their daily work.'[2] The predominant orientation to work was the instrumental one. As wage earners they were in effect 'selling their labour power, by the hour or "piece" in a market situation'. Workers in all groups tended to be 'motivated to increase their power as consumers and their domestic standard of living rather than their satisfaction as producers and the degree of their self-fulfilment in work'.[3] The craftsmen in the sample had more in common with the white-collar workers than with the shop-floor men. They expected intrinsic satisfactions from their work as well as extrinsic economic ones and experienced frustration when these expectations were not satisfied. This happened notably 'in regard to their desire for autonomy and responsibility and for the conditions they believe essential for good workmanship'.[4]

Wedderburn and Crompton report a similar finding in a later study.[5] After discussing the similarities between the views of tradesmen and general workers over welfare schemes and amenities and the importance of pay and good working conditions, they go on to say, 'In other respects, however, the attitudes of tradesmen and general workers diverged sharply. The tradesmen did not value highly the security of employment offered by the Company. But this did not mean that they did not feel secure. The difference lay in the fact that their confidence was founded on the belief that their own skills *earned* their security, not that they were dependent upon a particular

[1] Vol. 1, ibid., p. 1.   [2] Vol. 1, ibid., p. 144.
[3] Vol. 1, ibid., p. 38.   [4] Vol. 1, ibid., p. 37.
[5] Wedderburn, Dorothy and Crompton, Rosemary, *Workers' Attitudes and Technology*, C.U.P., 1972.

employer. Consequently they were less committed to the Company and expressed a willingness to move if "something better turned up" and many were looking or had looked for other jobs. They were less likely than the general workers to find their jobs boring. Indeed, they *expected* interesting work and were frustrated when they did not find it. They were more sensitive than the general workers to gradations of status within the Company and many felt that their own work contribution was undervalued. This constellation of attitudes can be termed "craft consciousness". It was this craft consciousness which supplied the tradesmen with a sense of self worth which was significantly lacking among the general workers which led them to take a broader view of many problems than the general workers. They had more decided attitudes on most questions and they were also aware, at least, of the problems of the lower paid semi-skilled worker. But their first concern was with their own position. The very frustration expressed by the tradesmen when they felt their ability to do "a good job" was being interfered with, and the readiness with which they took action to protect "their" craft indicates the importance which they attached to their own sense of identity.'[1]

As we have seen these comments are certainly applicable to the craftsmen interviewed in this study and also in a somewhat different context to the technicians. Many respondents who complained either about their working conditions, their lack of promotion or the difficulties of part-time study were nevertheless self-confident and felt that their training and their attendance at college courses had been thoroughly worth while. For example, 327 (80 per cent) of them rated the years at college 'worth while for personal satisfaction' (Table 6.8, p. 101) whereas in comments on their college careers only 33 per cent had 'no regrets' (Table 5.10, p. 82) and less than 50 per cent had gained a recognised certificate[2] (Table 5.7, p. 75).

Finally some reference should be made to the work of a group of Aston researchers under the leadership of D. S. Pugh. In an early paper[3] in which they set out their plans they make the point that previous studies of work organisation and behaviour fell into two groups: they were concerned either with administrative processes or the processes of group interaction. They quote Bennis who

[1] Ibid., pp. 142–3.
[2] A further 8 per cent had passed an Intermediate Examination of the City and Guilds.
[3] Pugh, D. S. et al., 'A Conceptual Scheme for Organisational Analysis', *Administrative Science Quarterly*, 1963, Vol. 8, No. 3, pp. 289–315.

categorised the first group who studied organisation structure and functioning as being concerned with 'organisations without people'[1] and the human-relations group as being concerned with 'people without organisations'. 'There has been almost no systemic exploration of the causal connection between contextual factors and certain administrative systems rather than others, or certain group and individual behaviours rather than others.'[2]

The Aston plan therefore was to study work organisation and behaviour by means of three conceptually distinct levels of analysis: (1) organisational structure and functioning; (2) group composition and interaction; (3) individual personality and behaviour; and to use factorial analysis to study the interrelations between each of the levels. 'Thus for example, we aim to study a particular level of analysis, say group composition and interaction, systematically *in relation to* particular organisational structures, not as so often in the past, in neglect of them.'[3]

They started by separating activity variables from structural ones on the grounds that the empirical study of an organisation can only be carried out in relation to the activities which arise from its many processes. The list of activity variables is in effect a description of the basic resources of an organisation including, for example, people, materials, money, ideas and so on. To examine the structural variables they compiled a list of six primary dimensions of organisational structure and set about devising a set of scales which could be operationally defined for all the six variables: (1) specialisation, (2) standardisation, (3) formalisation, (4) centralisation, (5) configuration and (6) flexibility. The one which relates particularly to the educational and training activities of a firm is the second – standardisation – and it is because this group of research workers intended to include a consideration of the educational and training policies of organisations that their plans are reported here in some detail. Standardisation of procedures and of roles are the two aspects of this dimension which are considered. The paragraph on roles must be quoted in full.

'Standardisation of *roles* is concerned with the degree to which the organisation prescribes the standardisation of (1) role definition and qualifications for office (2) role-performance measurement (3)

---

[1] Bennis, W. G., 'Leadership Theory and Administrative Behaviour', *Administrative Science Quarterly*, 1959, Vol. 4, pp. 259–301.

[2] Pugh et al., ibid., p. 291.

[3] Ibid., p. 293.

titles for office and symbols of role status and (4) rewards for role-performance. Underlying these scales is the degree to which either achievement or ascriptive attributes are taken into account. This is at the base of Weber's distinction between bureaucratic and traditional forms of organisation. As Bendix has insightfully pointed out, in modern organisation the opposite of bureaucratic insistence on achievement attributes is the stress on personality characteristics: "It doesn't matter what qualifications he's got, as long as he's a sound chap who will fit into our organisation."[1]

In the event, the comment made by Bennis – and echoed by many other observers[2] – was not disproven. They had trouble devising a 'qualifications' scale because so few managers knew what the qualifications of their subordinates were and the 'training specialisation' scale which they devised could not be used to predict what training specialists a firm would employ because the categories were not endorsed in any ascending order.[3] It should be noted however that this work was done before the Industrial Training Act. Of the 52 organisations studied, 31 employed no training specialists. In 15 of the remaining 21 most of the specialists were instructors for manual work. What relationships did exist were overshadowed by the much larger relationships between size and the overall 'structuring of activities'. A familiar story.

The follow-up study, based as it is on day-release technical college students, is limited, as far as employers are concerned, to those who allowed at least some of their workers to study during working hours. Even so, feedback from the respondents confirms that illogicalities and inconsistencies are not hard to find, especially among firms with less than 1,000 employees

There were some positive results from the 1960 study to justify the attempt to seek further information in this area. In the analysis of success and failure, measured ability was held constant by calculating, instead of a pass rate, an 'achievement ratio'. This was the pass rate for those 'capable' of passing: capability being statistically determined by the use of appropriate test scores and the method of 'least misfits'.

The overall achievement ratio in the first year was 79 per cent and the range between the various courses was from 100 per cent down

---

[1] Pugh et al., ibid., p. 303.   [2] See reference to Blaug et al., p. 15.
[3] I am indebted to Miss Diana C. Pheysey, Research Fellow, Industrial Administration, The University of Aston in Birmingham, for a personal communication on this topic.

to 55 per cent. In two trade courses concerned with site-contracting work – Heating and Ventilating Engineering and Radio and Television Servicing – all students with scores above the cut-off passed i.e. they had a ratio of 100 per cent. In each case (i) there was a good 'match' between college study and the work 'on the job' and (ii) the practitioners were providing a service for individual clients in which there is a need for safety precautions. These particular employers thus had a vested interest in the certification of technical competence. The superior performance of these two groups continued over the following three years.

The other vector, which in earlier studies was shown to be connected with college success, was size of firm. The important distinguishing feature between the smaller and the larger firms was not so much actual examination success but persistence in the examination stakes. 'Over the years those persisting belong in growing proportions to the large firms: conversely among the drop-outs the small firms are over-represented.'[1] Procedures governing education and training are of course more formalised in large undertakings and the 'privilege' of day release is unlikely to be withdrawn capriciously. Conversely any withdrawal from college attendance would not pass unnoticed. However the 'rules' can vary – some firms allowing release for five years – the minimum time necessary for an H.N.C. or a full technical certificate of the City and Guilds or three years geared to the time necessary for O.N.C.

We return therefore to consider the three organisational variables used on the questionnaire – size of firm, type of firm and scale of production (already discussed in Chapter 4) – comparing them first with the recognition according to college success within the organisations and secondly with the level of success actually obtained. The results are set out in Tables 6.9 to 6.14.

Just over half the students in large firms reported some form of recognition for college success; among the rest it was 39 per cent (Table 6.9). This was unlikely to have arisen by chance but the overlap is of course considerable. Taken together, over half the sample reported 'no recognition' for success at college.

In Table 6.10 it is clear that the largest firms were not superior to category III (250–999) in terms of college achievement. If the two smallest groups are compared with the two largest, differences are highly significant. In the former 14 per cent of respondents ($\frac{9}{64}$) reached H.N.C. and beyond and in the latter 21 per cent ($\frac{51}{245}$). In

[1] *The Young Worker at College*, ibid., p. 155.

TABLE 6.9
Size of firm by recognition of success O.N.C. respondents

Column percentages

	Size of firm by number of employees					
	I, II and III 999 and below		IV 1000 +		Totals	
	N	%	N	%	N	%
No recognition	52	61	65	47	117	53
Some: e.g. bonus or increased wages or promotion	33	39	72	53	105	47
Totals	85	100	137	100	222	100
Row percentages	38		62		100	

Chi sq. $=4.07$ $p < 0.05$
Results for trade entrants were identical. Taken together value of Chi sq. increases to 6.62 $p = 0.01$.

TABLE 6.10

Size of firm by achievement after twenty-one O.N.C. respondents

Column percentages

Achievement after 21	Size of firm by number of employees									
	I 99 and below		II 100–249		III 250–999		IV 1000 +		Totals	
	N	%	N	%	N	%	N	%	N	%
(1) Less than (2)	14	46	11	32	27	44	76	41	128	41
(2) O.N.C. final	9	30	15	44	16	26	60	33	100	32
(3) First year H.N.C.	2	6	4	12	3	5	12	6	21	7
(4) H.N.C. and beyond	5	16	4	12	15	25	36	19	60	19
Totals	30	100	34	100	61	100	184	100	309	100
Row percentages	10		11		20		59		100	

Comparing Firms I and II with III and IV on the two extreme achievement ratings

25	103
9	51

Chi sq. $= 11.4$ $p < 0.001$

111

Table 6.11
Type of firm by recognition of success O.N.C. respondents

Column percentages

Recognition	Type of firm																
	Manufacturing										Contractors		Public Bodies		Totals	
	(a)		(b)		(c)		Others		Totals							
	N	%	N	%	N	%	N	%	N	%	N	%	N	%	N	%
None	16	43	31	52	74	49	10	53	131	49	16	64	16	59	163	51
Some: e.g. bonus or increased wages or promotion	21	57	29	48	77	51	9	47	136	51	9	36	11	41	156	49
Totals	37	100	60	100	151	100	19	100	267	100	25	100	27	100	319	100
Row percentages	12		19		47		6		84		<8		>8		100	

(a) = small articles, few components; (b) = small articles, many components; (c) = large articles, many components.
49 per cent of respondents in Manufacturing firms reported that no rewards were made for college achievement and over 61 per cent from the other two types of firm ($\frac{32}{52}$), but with the small numbers involved in Contracting firms and Public Bodies the differences did not reach a statistically significant level

$$\frac{131}{136} \quad \bigg| \quad \frac{32}{20}$$

Chi sq. = 2·66 p >0·1

With four times as many in these other organisations the proportionate differences would give a Chi sq. of 7·4 and a 1 in 100 probability that they are not due to chance.

TABLE 6.12
Type of firm by achievement after twenty-one O.N.C. respondents

Column percentages

	Type of firm															
	Manufacturing [1]										Contractors		Public Bodies		Totals	
	(a)		(b)		(c)		Others		Totals							
Achievement after 21	N	%	N	%	N	%	N	%	N	%	N	%	N	%	N	%
(1) Less than (2)	29	51	36	41	65	34	12	46	142	39	19	50	27	61	188	42
(2) O.N.C. final	16	28	25	29	52	27	6	23	99	28	14	37	7	16	120	27
(3) First year H.N.C.	2	>3	5	6	20	11	1	4	28	8	0	0	1	2	29	7
(4) H.N.C. and beyond	10	<18	21	24	53	28	7	27	91	25	5	13	9	21	105	24
Totals	57	100	87	100	190	100	26	100	360	100	38	100	44	100	442	100
Row percentages	13		20		43		6		<82		>8		10		100	

[1] See key in Table 6.11.

Comparing Manufacturing with the rest on the Extreme achievement ratings

142	46
91	14

Chi sq. = 5.13   p = 0.025

Comparing Manufacturing (type c) with all other manufacturing on extreme ratings

65	77
54	48

Chi sq. = 3.4   p > 0.05

this sample we are of course dealing with the 'persisters' in all types of firm as is clear from Table 5.15 in the previous chapter, p. 89.

As we saw in Chapter 4,[1] three-quarters of the respondents were employed in manufacturing industry so that differences between these organisations and the other quarter have to be very large to reach a statistically significant level (Table 6.11). There is some interaction with size. For example, most of the firms manufacturing small articles with few components such as screws and metal castings (Type (a)) are large and they had the largest percentage (57) recognising college success. In the other categories the relationship with

TABLE 6.13

Scale of production by recognition of success
O.N.C. respondents

Column percentages

Scale of production: manufacturing industry only

Recognition	(a) One-offs		(b) Large batch		(c) Mass production		(d) Continuous flow		Others		Totals	
	N	%	N	%	N	%	N	%	N	%	N	%
None	43	44	33	65	36	45	2	29	17	49	131	49
Some	54	56	18	35	44	55	5	71	18	51	139	51
Totals	97	100	51	100	80	100	7	100	35	100	270	100
Row percentages	<36		19		30		>2		13		100	

Large batch production negatively and significantly related to recognition of college success.

$$\frac{33\ \ |\ \ 98}{18\ \ |\ \ 121} \quad \text{Chi sq.} = 6\cdot67 \quad p = 0\cdot01$$

43 per cent of respondents occupied on large batch processes were in the smaller firms. For one-offs, where over half had some recognition of academic achievement, 52 per cent were in smaller firms (cf. Appendix III, Table A6·1, p. 178). This suggests that small firms manufacturing prototypes to individual specification are more likely to value technical college achievement than firms engaged in large batch production.

[1] Table 4.2, p. 51.

114

TABLE 6.14

**Scale of production by achievement after twenty-one
O.N.C. respondents**

Column percentages

| Achievement after 21 | Scale of production | | | | | | | | | | |
| | (a) One-offs Small batch | | (b) Large batch | | (c) Mass production | | (d) Continuous flow | | Others | | Totals | |
	N	%	N	%	N	%	N	%	N	%	N	%
(1) Less than (2)	50	38	32	43	34	35	5	42	22	47	143	40
(2) O.N.C. final	29	22	24	32	29	30	5	42	12	26	99	27
(3) First- year H.N.C.	10	8	5	7	11	11	0	0	2	4	28	8
(4) H.N.C. & beyond	42	32	13	18	23	24	2	16	11	23	91	25
Totals	131	100	74	100	97	100	12	100	47	100	361	100
Row percentages	36		21		27		3		13		100	

Among those succeeding at H.N.C. level (1st year and beyond) workers in Large batch and Continuous flow production were under represented.

$$\frac{66 \mid 142}{20 \mid 86}$$ Chi sq. $= 5 \cdot 84$ $p > 0 \cdot 02$

size is not straightforward. In category (b) (small articles with many components) only about a quarter of the sample was in large firms and in category (c) (large articles), where rewards were only marginally more plentiful, about three-quarters came from large firms.

When type of firm is related to actual achievement (Table 6.12) differences are greater and the manufacturing firms as a whole had significantly more students reaching H.N.C. standard than the others. Over 61 per cent of O.N.C. students employed by Public Bodies, which were all large, failed to reach O.N.C. finals. Within the manufacturing groups, Type (c) had 39 per cent of its students going on beyond O.N.C. compared with 27 per cent for the rest.

Three organisational variables – size and type of firm and scale of production in manufacturing firms – have been examined in relation to (i) the learner's opinion of the training he received (Tables 4.15– 4.17, pp. 62–4); (ii) the firm's recognition of the learner's college success (Tables 6.9, 6.11 and 6.13 above) and (iii) the learner's achievement at college (Tables 6.10, 6.12 and 6.14).

The overriding influence of the size of the employing firm in relation to technical education is confirmed once again: the training given in larger firms is rated more highly, they are more likely to reward the successful student/worker and the student/worker is more likely to be successful. In the analysis of the two other variables – type of firm and scale of production – the interaction with size complicates the picture and this requires detailed study preferably within the firms themselves. There are also two other areas in which the findings might repay further investigation.

First, the respondents working for contracting firms and for public bodies were more likely to have a high opinion of the training provided than those in manufacturing industry, despite the fact that these two types of organisation gave fewer rewards for academic study and their students were less persistent and less successful. A possible explanation is that 'on the job' training is often on a one to one, man and boy, basis which is felt to be more satisfying. The apparent lack of college success was due in some of these cases to transfer from the O.N.C. course to trade courses more closely geared to the job in the firm.

The second set of differences worthy of comment relate to those between respondents who joined manufacturing firms engaged in large batch production and the others employed in manufacturing industries. A larger proportion had a low opinion of the training facilities; fewer firms in the large batch category offered rewards for college work and their students were less successful academically.

One of the main concerns of the organisational theorists already mentioned is the relationship between workers' attitudes and the technology of the process in which they are engaged. The relation-ship is far from simple: 'large batch production', for example, is a phrase covering a wide variety of situations and products, so that it would be impossible to find a simple phrase to sum up the workers' attitudes. The book by Joan Woodward, *Industrial Organisation:*

Theory and Practice, has a useful chapter on 'The Planning and Control of Production'.[1] Writing of 'Batch and Intermittent Production' she indicates the difficulty of defining objectives precisely: such work, she says, is generally discussed in terms of 'maximisation of profit', 'quick customer service', 'as high an output as possible'. This element of uncertainty can lead to complex control procedures and uneasy relationships between those responsible for the administration of production and those responsible for the supervision of production operations. Confusion arises also when subsidiary objectives become difficult or impossible to reconcile with each other. 'In most of these firms, the master plan was more of a myth than a reality.' 'In batch and intermittent production, on the whole, the identification which develops spontaneously in other types of production can only be brought about through conscious and deliberate effort by the top management.'[2] Several attributes which make for a feeling of satisfaction in work are often lacking: it is generally difficult for the individual worker to comprehend the whole process and he has little control over the work he has to do.

The tables in this chapter which involve organisational variables relate to the firms in which the respondents had spent the first few years of their working life. Very few had remained on the shop floor and about half had moved to another firm, the nature of which was not recorded. The findings pose some questions which a retrospective study of this kind cannot possibly answer. What is needed is a two-pronged investigation of several groups of young workers in a variety of industrial settings (a) during their periods on the job, and (b) during their time at the local college. The educational variable in the policies of employers may be even more difficult to disentangle than the technological ones, but the quest should not be abandoned.

[1] Ibid., Chapter 9, pp. 154–81.   [2] Ibid., p. 171.

CHAPTER 7

The Social Effects of Technical College Achievement

Putting your boy 'to a trade' or 'signing him on' for an apprenticeship has been the recognised way for a labouring couple to help a son to succeed in life ever since we became an industrial nation. It involved hardship because the money was poor at first but the expectation was that he would never be without work and would be 'a cut above' the labourer. An apprenticeship or other learnership is a step or two up the ladder and in so far as the colleges have been, throughout their history, involved in the education and training of such young workers they too are seen as instruments of upward mobility. They were not, however, specifically designed for this purpose, nor is it their sole function. They also serve a 'cooling out' function[1] for young people who are unable to match the expectations and/or performance of their parents. While they provide opportunities for those moving upwards, they also soften the blow for those who are downwardly mobile. Their clientele thus produce an interesting social mix which has become increasingly complex in the last decade or so. The colleges have had to face new situations for which they were in no way prepared – in terms of staff or accommodation for example – and their response, though patchy, has in some instances been exciting and imaginative.

The question of the future role of the colleges is discussed in the final chapter: here we are concerned with the effect of college experience on the social status of their industrially based students. The first section of the questionnaire provided information on father's job and son's job (on the Nelson seven-point scale) and by subtracting the son's score from the father's a mobility scale was constructed which was reduced to three points: lower, same and higher.

---

[1] See Clark, Burton R., 'The "Cooling Out" Function in Higher Education', *Amer. J. Sociol.*, Vol. LXV, 1960. cf. *The Young Worker at College*, ibid., p. 224.

The two direct questions in Section IV – asking for the opinions of the respondents on their educational experiences and their opportunities for finding a job to their liking – have been dealt with in Chapter 3[1] where there is also some discussion of the difficulty of interpreting responses to a 'satisfaction' scale since they are bound to be linked with expectations and the self-image. The other two questions in this section were therefore open-ended avoiding a head-on attack. About half the respondents rated their opportunities for finding a job as satisfactory (195 O.N.C. and 96 trade respondents in Table 3.9, p. 38): the other half were then asked what improvements they would like to see for their own sons.[2] This was based on the supposition that most parents want to provide better opportunities for their children than those they have themselves enjoyed and that responses therefore would indirectly reflect their own dissatisfactions. Similarly, the final question was concerned with the educational opportunities they wanted for their own children and no lead was given to predetermine the response.

Tables 7.1–7.4 deal first with the mobility scale. Among the trade

TABLE 7.1

Mobility: Differences in level between father's job and son's

		Lower		Same		Higher	
Sample	N	N	%	N	%	N	%
O.N.C. respondents	416	54[4]	13·0	114	27·4	248[4]	59·6
Trade respondents	180	41[4]	22·8	56	31·1	83[4]	46·1
O.N.C. interviewees	106	11	10·4	33	31·1	62	58·5
Trade interviewees	47	11	23·4	12	25·5	24	51·1

students about half had improved on the level of their father's job, for the O.N.C. students the figure is nearer 60 per cent. Again for the O.N.C. sample significantly fewer fell *below* the father's job level even though more of their fathers were in the higher categories.[3]

[1] pp. 37–45.
[2] Respondents frequently mentioned daughters and the designer of the questionnaire was quite rightly attacked on the grounds of sexual discrimination.
[3] Cf. Table 3.6, p. 35.
[4] Chi squared $= 11·04$ $p = 0·001$.

In the total samples the ages of the respondents i.e. the sons, ranged from 32·8 to 22·6 years: thus some were just beginning their careers and others had probably reached their ceiling. Table 7.2 gives the breakdown into the four cohorts of 106 O.N.C. respondents in the interview sample. As would be expected the proportion reaching higher levels of job goes up with age but in this sample (randomised to be representative of all subjects at risk) there is little evidence of further change in relation to father's job beyond the early thirties.

TABLE 7.2

Mobility: O.N.C. interviewees (Table 7.1) according to age

| Cohorts | N | % | Mean age in 1966 | Son's job in relation to father's was: | | |
				Lower %	Same %	Higher %
1960	23	100	22·6	8·7	39·1	52·2
1957	53	100	25·8	17·0	24·5	58·5
1952	19	100	30·7	0	36·8	62·2
1950	11	100	32·8	0	36·4	63·6
Totals	106 9 NK[1]	100		10·4	31·1	58·5

In Table 7.3 the 1957 cohort is again used for detailed analysis since it is the largest sample taking similar courses in any one age group and also has the additional advantage of occupying the middle position with regard to age. It also provides a reminder that the son's mobility is not being judged from a very low baseline. Only 10 per cent of the fathers were semi- or unskilled workers.

The figures given in Table 7.4 show a highly significant relationship between succeeding at college and improving on the father's position. However, an H.N.C. does not make the son upwardly mobile if his father is in a professional position and 6 per cent, though 'qualified' in terms of college achievement, had lower status jobs than their fathers.

The next table – 7.5 – collects together the comments of those dissatisfied with their own opportunities for finding a job into nine categories and is self-explanatory.

[1] NK = not known.

TABLE 7.3

Son's mobility scale by father's job level
1957 cohort

Column percentages

N = 223   13 Not known = 5·5% of 236

Son's job in relation to father's was:

Father's job level	Lower %	Same %	Higher %	Totals %	N	All O.N.C.s %	N
Professional	54	35	0	19	42	15	64
Highly Skilled	40	47	21	32	71	>30	128
Skilled and Moderately Skilled	6	<17	62	39	88	44	183
Semi- and Unskilled	0	>1	17	10	22	> 10	44
Totals %	100	100	100	100		100	
Totals N	35	66	122	223			419
Row percentages	<16	>29	55	100			
All O.N.C. respondents N	54	114	251				419
Row percentages	13	27	60				100

526 respondents (82 per cent) answered the final question on the education of their offspring and of these 87 (17 per cent) dealt only with schooling and the selective versus comprehensive problem. The rest of the replies fell readily into two sections: well over half wanted more full-time education at school and at a university or on sand-wich courses in colleges. The rest felt they would be content with the present system provided that it could be improved – better training, more block release, closer contact between firm and college and so on. For the randomised samples the response rate was converted to 100 per cent as this topic was discussed at some length during the interviews. The few who had not written an answer on the form had no hesitation in expressing themselves on the subject – often forcefully – when we met. Most of the rest endorsed and enlarged upon what they had already written.

TABLE 7.4
Mobility by achievement after twenty-one
1957 cohort

Column percentages

Achievement after 21	Son's job in relation to father's was:			Totals		All O.N.C.s	
	Lower	Same	Higher	%	N	%	N
1. Less than 2	77	44	34	44	98	43	179
2. O.N.C. final; C. & G. 5th year	17	36	29	29	65	27	113
3. First-year H.N.C.	0	5	9	6	14	6	26
4. H.N.C. final and above	6	15	28	21	46	24	101
Totals % N	100 35	100 66	100 122	100	223	100	419
Row percentages	<16	>29	55	100			
All O.N.C. respondents	54	114	251				419
Row percentages	13	27	60				100

	Lower and Same	Higher
1 and 2	86	77
3 and 4	15	45

Chi sq. = 13·6
p <0·0005

TABLE 7.5

Question: If not satisfied with your opportunities for finding a job, what improvements would you like to see for your own sons?

Type of comment		Samples							
		Total respondents		Total interviewees		O.N.C. respondents		O.N.C. interviewees	
		N	%	N	%	N	%	N	%
Schools should be more in touch with industry and its requirements	1.	36	13·2	14	18·2	26	12·6	10	17·5
There should be more career talks and/or industrial visits	2.	61	22·3	9	11·7	49	23·8	9	15·8
More understanding by management of the problems of junior staff	3.	14	5·1	7	9·1	11	5·3	6	10·5
It would not be in my son's own interest to follow in my footsteps – easier ways of earning money	4.	32	11·7	10	13·0	27	13·1	6	10·5
There should be greater contact between Youth Employment Offices and schools	5.	31	11·4	5	6·5	21	10·2	2	3·5
No favouritism – jobs on merit and ability	6.	31	11·4	13	16·9	26	12·6	10	17·5
Should be trained for a job before leaving school	7.	41	15·0	13	16·9	26	12·6	10	17·5
There should be centres where different types of jobs could be demonstrated	8.	26	9·5	5	6·5	19	9·2	3	5·3
More attention should be paid to the lesser-known industries	9.	1	0·4	1	1·3	1	0·5	1	1·8
Totals		273[1]	100·0	77	100·1	206[1]	99·9	57	99·9

[1] Cf. Table 3.8, page 37 in which 211 O.N.C. respondents and 77 of the trade group were less than satisfied.

In Table 7.6 the replies for the interview sample are analysed according to the level of achievement of the respondent. 64 per cent of those dealing with post-school education wanted it to be full-time at a university or college and among the 25 per cent who had continued to study beyond the O.N.C. stage, 78 per cent wanted full-time provision for their own children. Even among those with minimal achievement, which included most of the trade students who were interviewed, the proportion was well over half.

TABLE 7.6

Question: If you have, now or in the future, a son of your own, would you say whether and in what way, you would like his educational opportunities to differ from your own

Education of children by final level of father's college achievement

Total interview sample
Percentages

Post-school education for their children	1. Less than 2	2. O.N.C. or final C. &. G.	3. More than 2.	Totals[1]
More full-time university	59	62	78[2]	64
Present system with improvements	41	38	22	36
Totals	100	100	100	100
N	85	26	37	148
Non-selective schooling	9	6	3	18
Total sample	94	32	40	166
%	57	19	24	100

It is worth while reiterating that at no time did the interviewees receive any hint about possible ways of dealing with this question: a few verbatim examples of their spontaneous replies are appended.

'School to eighteen – perhaps a sandwich course at a university.' Why? 'The university lads I know come out much more confident' (than I am). 'If you're pushed into a works at fifteen it's a shock. With a sandwich course you get the best of both worlds.'

'Obviously full-time is better than the way I've done it.' 'I go

[1] See Table A7.6, page 180, for the comparable figures for the other samples.
[2] The comparable figure for the total respondents sample was 76 per cent, a difference which is statistically negligible.

to college one day a week and I haven't a clue what I did seven days ago. It calls for such a lot of work at home and when you're married this is difficult. Married, new home, study three nights a week – it's a lot at once.'

'Naturally they've got to stay at school to get "A" levels. Block-release courses a good idea – devote all your time to it – not divided as I've been.'

'Day-release and evening type training is out. If I'd had "A" levels . . . much easier.'

'There's a definite waste of talent in this country. Young men of thirteen or fourteen don't realise what education is all about. I'll campaign for full-time higher education for any son I have.'

'My son will have full-time university education – Definitely!'

'Nothing to beat "A" levels and university. Gives a chap confidence – that kind of education is accepted. They can be referred in one subject – the H.N.C. chaps can't.'

Finally, one who was 'lucky enough' to get on a Dip.Tech. course.

'I failed S_2 twice but then the firm helped me to get on the O.N.D. (full-time) course. Got 91 per cent in the examination and that got me on to a Dip.Tech. I saw my chance and seized it but it's all so chancy.'

Parental pressure on children to do well at school and 'get on' is so universal that it seems hardly necessary to monitor it. Accounts of family journeys from working-class to middle- and even upper-class status – 'clogs to riches' – are commonplace even if sometimes apocryphal. There have been many studies in this area.[1] An American writing in 1953, defended the 'obvious' nature of such findings by the claim that they would 'throw much light on and hence aid the solution of, a delicate problem which has to be faced by every classroom teacher: how to cope with the influence of parents' attitudes on the motivation and behaviour of their children'.[2] The important question is what are the social influences which motivate young people to heed their parents' wishes and what is it that

[1] See for example Martin, F. W., 'An Enquiry into Parents' Preferences in Secondary Education' in Glass, D. V. (Ed.), *Social Mobility in Britain*, Routledge & Kegan Paul, 1954; and Turner, R. H., 'Sponsored and Contest Mobility and the School System' reprinted in Halsey, Floud and Anderson (Eds.), *Education, Economy and Society*, Free Press of Glencoe, 1961.

[2] Kahl, Joseph A., 'Educational and Occupational Aspirations of "Common Man" Boys', *Harvard Educational Review*, Vol. XXIII, No. 3, Summer 1953.

accounts for the differences which are apparent to everyone and particularly noticeable among part-time day release students.

Goldthorpe in his study of *embourgeoisement*[1] examined the aspirations of his 'affluent workers' for their children, educationally and occupationally. Their responses were only at a slightly lower level than those from his control sample of white-collar workers and his group was indeed more 'ambitious' than those interviewed in other studies e.g. that of J. W. B. Douglas in *The Home and the School*.[2] He discusses the 'meaning' of these ambitions and also reports that an examination of the records of the children already in secondary school or employment showed that 'the discrepancy between parental ambitions and children's performance is often quite striking.'[3]

This warning note must clearly be heeded in any interpretation of the results reported here. In the context of promotion prospects he makes the point that 'aspirations may be held with little conviction as to their plausibility' and argues on the basis of contrasts in attitude between his manual and white-collar samples that 'the middle class conception of "getting on" through a career can be of little relevance in relation to the typical life-chances of largely *unqualified* [my italics] rank and file industrial workers.'[4]

There are many similarities between the two samples. All the respondents to this study were 'unqualified' school leavers: most of those interviewed were married and about half the interviews took place at home where almost invariably I met the wife and often the children too. Most of them were buying houses in modern estates and the cost of mortgages and of children were common ground between them. They too, like Goldthorpe's subjects, were on the whole home-based, tied to wife and family and had relatively few social contacts outside and, as I have already remarked, my visit was often welcomed for social reasons. However, in any list of criteria on which people are stratified socially, occupational achievement and education are likely to find a place and one possibly crucial difference between Goldthorpe's sample and this one is the educational component.

Aspirations for their children among our respondents were based largely on their own educational experience and a large number were disillusioned with the route they had travelled and wanted an easier and surer route to middle-class status for their own children.

[1] Ibid., p. 132.　　　　[2] London, 1967.
[3] Goldthorpe et al., Vol. 3, ibid., p. 134.　　　[4] Ibid., p. 123.

The well-established National Certificate system, which in the past provided the bulk of our qualified engineers, was no longer acceptable to them. It was lengthy, hazardous and moreover no longer highly regarded as a status symbol. Those who hope to keep part-time education of this kind alive on grounds of cheapness, are likely to meet opposition from frustrated parents and will need to introduce and re-introduce some radical reforms – such as, for example, open access, at the top end, to chartered status, credit systems, more block-release and government grants.

It is ironic, if understandable, that at the moment when pressure on full-time places in colleges and universities is increasing, the part-time route is being made more difficult, by the professional institutions who are closing their doors and by the operation of the Industrial Training Act which has virtually brought to an end release of workers for their own individual educational purposes. The day when technicians will be pass degree men is fast approaching the eastern shores of the Atlantic.

CHAPTER 8

The Local Tech. in the 1970s

At the time of writing many of the local technical colleges are in the doldrums squeezed between the schools which are retaining more of the sixteen- to eighteen-year-olds in their sixth forms and the universities and other institutions of higher education which are attracting more and more of the eighteen to twenty-one age group into full-time study.

The promised increase in part-time and block-release students from industry predicted at the time of the passing of the Industrial Training Act has not taken place. What increases have come the way of the colleges have, on the whole, been either in courses traditionally associated with the schools such as 'O' and 'A' level Certificates of Education or in full-time 'off the job' training courses which were previously provided 'on the job' by the firms. National Certificate and other technical courses, a major commitment of the local techs., have diminished.

In this chapter we review the events of the past eight years which preceded the present stalemate and follow it with a discussion of possible outcomes in the final chapter.

The Industrial Training Act was passed in 1964 and had three main objectives:

    (i) to enable discussions on the scale of training to be better related to economic needs and technological developments;

    (ii) to improve the overall quality of industrial training and to establish minimum standards; and

    (iii) to enable the cost to be more fairly spread.[1]

The proposals as set out in the White Paper quoted above involved the further education colleges only in the relatively minor role of providing 'associated further education' but the Central Training

[1] *Industrial Training: Government Proposals*, Cmnd. 1892, H.M.S.O., December 1962.

Council in its reports has usually included some hopeful phrase about educational provision. For example the following passage is taken from its Second Report to the Minister.[1]

... in the last year, there has been some evidence that many employers have felt disinclined because of the general economic situation to release people to attend courses of further education at the Colleges. We are *none the less confident* that the boards' measures will before long *encourage* a very much wider use of college facilities. (My italics.)

The following year the C.T.C. gave its own version of the aims of the Act in terms considerably different from those of the Act itself:

to ensure that enough workers with the requisite skills are available in the right places at the right time to do efficiently the jobs needing to be done.

to provide better opportunities to individuals to develop their skills and use their abilities to the full.[2]

Criticisms from both industrialists and educators have led the Government to review the working of the Act and put forward proposals for a change in the law. The introduction to these proposals contains a clear unequivocal statement on the subject of industrial training:

Training is not an end in itself. Skills are only useful to the economy and beneficial to the individual when they can be effectively employed. Training – even good training – will not necessarily pay off unless it is directed to real needs. Nor is additional training necessarily the only way of dealing with an apparent shortage of skilled workers. It may be possible to use existing skills more effectively. Nevertheless, there is ample evidence that investment in improved training can pay off for firms, for individuals and for the community.[3]

In the light of this statement and of the emphasis in the publications of the training boards on the need for *effective* training, the introduction by the C.T.C. of the idea of 'better opportunities to individuals ... to use their abilities to the full' cannot be regarded as

[1] H.M.S.O. 1967, p. 15, para. 38. See also *Review of the Central Training Council*, Cmnd. 4335, H.M.S.O., 1970, para. 32, p. 10.
[2] See *Training for the Future – a Plan for Discussion*, Department of Employment, February 1972, p. 6.   [3] Ibid., p. 4. See note p. 141.

anything more than a sop to the educators who constitute about a quarter of their membership.

Young people leaving school at sixteen and starting work are not all going to be able unaided to discover what their abilities are, let alone use them to the full. Without imaginative effort, supported by new legislation, their educational opportunities will inevitably be restricted and many of us wish it could be otherwise. Hence the pious hopes which find their way into the literature on industrial training, into documents which, apart from a little lip-service to educational interests, deal in rational propositions.[1]

The reality is that we all – individuals as well as corporations – act in ways which produce a pay-off. Individuals are often content with an emotional reward without thought of material gain but for industrial concerns an emotional pay-off must come, if at all, *after* commercial success, not before. How could it be otherwise? Why do we, and particularly those of us in the education industry, go on imagining that this reified concept 'Industry' can be cajoled or 'encouraged' into accepting responsibility for the broader education of work people if the economic pay-off is non-existent?

The Act marks the end of paternalism in industry. the end of part-time day release granted as a privilege by the well-meaning employer. There are now twenty-seven Industrial Training Boards each responsible for identifying the training needs of its own group of industries and for initiating any appropriate changes in training practice. The operation is costed and the role of the colleges is to supply technical education 'associated' with the training demanded by the job. In the case of craftsmen they are in many cases providing the training as well. We know from experience that in trades where an educational component is seen by the employer as essential for the proper performance of the job, where formal certification is an insurance against possible harm to his customers, the necessary co-operation between employer, employee and technical teacher takes place. It was no accident that success rates in some trade courses were high and drop-out low, whereas in others the reverse was true. 'The law of the situation' ensured it.

---

[1] The writer herself fell into this trap on p. 217 of *The Young Worker at College*: 'Although the role of the technical college is not specified in the Act it is generally believed that the new Training Boards will want to make full use of them. It is certainly to be hoped that they will think of them as something more than "mere useful adjuncts to the workshop and the mine".' (Reference to Eustace Percy, *Education at the Crossroads*, Evans Bros., 1930, p. 57.)

Similar considerations apply to the dynamics of the local college. Not only was the young worker dependent upon industrial policies for his educational 'privileges', so also the local colleges have always been dependent upon their 'users'. They could only stay in business if local industrialists were prepared to 'support', i.e. release their young workers for, the courses they provided. Not only has the Industrial Training Act, despite the 'hopes', failed to give the colleges more say in the educational content of the courses, it has tended to increase their dependency. The relationship is now even less of a partnership and more of a 'mere adjunct'. Actual contact between college staffs and Training Officers may well have increased and certainly annual reports from the colleges are now pretty certain to contain sections headed 'Liaison with Industry', but such reports often convey the meaning of the word 'liaison' only too clearly. Here is one example: 'The College Advisory Panels met during the year when the advice given by representatives of employers and trade unions proved to be of real value to the College in planning and developing courses.' Perhaps 'The *Demands* of Industry' would be a clearer heading.

Other entries in similar reports read: '. . . there will be a growth in the development of courses devised by Training Boards which extend beyond the normal academic session of 36 weeks . . .' (in the context of a discussion on staffing problems).

'Firm X decided to follow an alternative course of education and training as laid down by the Y Industrial Training Board. This means that in future apprentices from X will follow [such and such a course] for the duration of the further education part. The College will also provide training for these apprentices for . . . It is *hoped* [my italics] that this new scheme will continue without alteration for a number of years and allow both staff and students to settle down to their work.' Firms A, B and C being less important 'users' of the college in question would naturally have to follow the dictates of Firm X or find another college.

Yet again, this time in connection with a quite different type of industry: 'This year, Firm Z, the main user of this course decided that in future a block release course would be more convenient for them. Arrangements were made therefore during the year, for the provision of block release courses in future sessions.' In another case 'enrolments in block release courses decreased sharply and will not be provided in future.'[1]

[1] I am indebted to several people who must remain anonymous for allowing me to read and quote from the annual reports of a number of local colleges.

The foregoing should not be read as carping criticism. The training courses devised by the I.T.B.s (which include members from the colleges) could well be an improvement in terms of efficient performance at work and the fact that block release is sometimes advantageous to the firm is of interest, but whatever the facts here, they should not blind us to the effect of the changes on the local colleges and the *educational* opportunities for young workers. Paternalism had its uses: many a young employee managed to use his day release to prepare for a future job rather than to improve his performance on the existing one and open access to the colleges for open-ended courses often made it possible for individuals to pursue their own interests in the employers' time. It was, however, as this study confirms, a very hit-or-miss affair and the tightening up and defining of industry's future role as a training rather than as an educational agency is to be welcomed. Paternalism and privileges are out-of-date concepts and we now have to face the fact not only that industrialists have implicitly refused to pay for any educational provision which is not a commercial necessity but that it is not educationally desirable that they should do so. It is becoming more and more generally recognised that to cope with the problems of the latter half of the twentieth century education beyond the age of sixteen is a *social* necessity. For this the suitable paymaster is the Government not industry or commerce. Two previous Education Acts – in 1917 and 1944 – made provision for part-time day release for all young workers but in each case the government of the day failed to implement this section. Next time the further education of the sixteen- to nineteen-year-olds should have high priority. Many people felt in 1964 that the Industrial Training Act was the wrong Act and that those concerned with education should have fought harder for educational legislation, but at least we now have a clearer idea of the problems to be solved. The role of industry in this area has been clarified by the Department of Employment and the ball is now firmly in the court of the Department of Education and Science. Whichever way they choose to play this ball the local colleges cannot fail to be involved. So, before considering some of the possible options, we turn to take a closer look at the present state of the colleges, eight years after the passing of the training Act.

Technical college resources. In 1964 it was confidently predicted that as a consequence of the Act there would be a large increase in enrolments and the colleges would be short of space. The National

Advisory Council on Education for Industry and Commerce set up a Committee on Technical College Resources with the following terms of reference:

> In the light of the expansion of their work now in hand, and the further demands which national developments are likely to place on them, to suggest ways of making the most effective use of the resources available and expected to become available in technical and other colleges of further education.[1]

With the introduction of industrial training boards over virtually the whole of British industry and commerce, further education in association with industrial training will be extended to large groups of young people who do not at present attend courses.[2]

The work of the industrial training boards will also stimulate the demand from students who are preparing for careers as technicians and technologists and in comparable jobs in non-technical occupations. Adults will attend the colleges in growing numbers for management, refresher and other courses after experience in industry. This is a need which as a nation we have scarcely begun to meet.[3]

This expected expansion did not take place and there has indeed been a decrease in some areas. Many reasons can be given and they have been discussed at length in the journals[4] but the fundamental issue about the difference between education and training, about the relationship between the local college and the local firm, is largely ignored. Table 8.1 is reproduced with permission from the Department of Employment[5] and shows that what increase in day release there has been since the passing of the Act was mainly among the eighteen- to twenty-year-old workers. Part of the increase is also due to the fact that colleges have undertaken to provide Industrial Training Courses where suitable facilities are not available in the

---

[1] Committee on Technical College Resources (Chairman, Sir Harry Pilkington, now Lord Pilkington). *Report on the Size of Classes and Approval of Further Education Courses*, National Advisory Council on Education for Industry and Commerce, 1966.

[2] Ibid., p. 4.   [3] Ibid., p. 5.

[4] The best source of references to these discussions is the B.A.C.I.E. Bibliography of publications in the field of education and training in industry. For a recent overview of the working of the Act, including plans for the future, see the report of the B.A.C.I.E. Conference, *Industrial Training – the Future*, British Association for Commercial and Industrial Education, 1972.

[5] Annex 5 p. 76 'Training for the Future', 1972. Source: D.E.S. *Statistics of Education*.

TABLE 8.1

ANNEX 5 Employees released for part-time further education at public sector and assisted establishments

England and Wales

Year	Age at 31 December 15–17					Age at 31 December 18–20			Age at 31 December 21 and over	All ages total
	Number in age group (000s)	Number insured as at June (000s)	Number on day- & block-release as at November (000s)	Percentage of age group on day- & block-release (%)	Percentage of number insured on day- & block-release (%)	Number in age group (000s)	Number on day- & block-release as at November (000s)	Percentage of age group on day- & block-release (%)	Number on day- & block-release as at November (000s)	Number on day- & block-release as at November (000s)
	1	2	3	4	5	6	7	8	9	10
1961	2115	1324[1]	250	12	19	1817	162	9	82	494
1962	2246	1398	261	12	19	1988	185	9	85	531
1963	2348	1456	269	11	18	2014	190	9	87	546
1964	2284	1453	276	12	19	2139	206	10	93	574
1965	2132	1355	269	13	20	2266	230	10	103	602
1966	2044	1225	265	13	21	2376	246	10	114	625
1967	1992	1157	261	13	23	2325	249	11	130	640
1968	1977	1072	255	13	24	2168	245	11	145	644
1969	1989	1022	253	13	25	2086	242	12	150	645
1970	1982	1019	244	12	24	2039	231	11	153	628

[1] As at May 1961.

Source: Department of Education and Science – *Statistics of Education*

local firms. Table 8.2 deals only with recruits to the engineering industry and is taken from statistics issued by the Engineering Industry Training Board.[1] It shows a steady decrease in numbers of trainees attending further education colleges both at craft and technician level between 1966 and 1970. Enrolments in National Certificate Courses show a similar picture. Table 8.3 has been compiled from D.E.S. Statistics of Further Education for the years 1968 and 1970 and shows an overall decrease in enrolments of 15 per cent at Ordinary levels and 13 per cent at the Higher levels.

The comparative figures for block-release and full-time i.e. Diploma courses are not impressive. At the Ordinary level 67 per cent are still on part-time day release with the remaining 33 per cent divided more or less equally between block-release and Diploma courses. The proportions at the Higher level are roughly 69 out of every 100 on part-time day, 28 on full-time Diploma courses and three on block release. 95 per cent of all O.N.C. block-release courses are in engineering.[2]

At Makinton Technical College which was the subject of the study reported in *The Young Worker at College* total day-time enrolments increased from approximately 2,500 in 1961 to just under 3,000 in 1970 and the figures for the following two years show a decrease. 'O' and 'A' level work which was non-existent in 1960 is now provided for about 300 students. The proportion of students on block release was around 3 per cent in 1962, increased to about 20 per cent by 1966 and showed a further overall increase to 24 per cent by 1970. This latest figure is due to changes of policy among electrical firms: in mechanical engineering classes there has been a sharp decrease in block-release enrolments since 1966.

D.E.S. statistics now provide figures for the number of students entering National Certificate examinations and numbers passing, though readers must calculate percentages for themselves. These have remained relatively unchanged throughout the 1960s. Just under two-thirds get through the Ordinary National Certificate examination and just over two thirds on the Diploma course. Table 8.4 has been compiled from figures given for electrical and mechanical engineering students on O.N.C. and O.N.D. courses between 1965 and 1970.

[1] *Report and Accounts*, 1970–1 (reproduced with the permission of the Controller of H.M.S.O.).
[2] D.E.S., *Statistics of Education, 1970*, Vol. 3, *Further Education*, p. 57, H.M.S.O., 1972.

TABLE 8.2[1]

Craft and technician trainees, including draughtsmen: estimated number completing the first year of training, 1966–67 to 1969–70

1	Craft trainees				Technician trainees			
	1966–67	1967–68	1968–69	1969–70	1966–67	1967–68	1968–69	1969–70
	2	3	4	5	6	7	8	9
Number following the Board's recommended first-year course of off-the-job training and further education	17,554	20,072	19,768	20,018	4,875	5,590	5,770	5,997
Number given other approved training	884	213	186	241	787	342	396	355
Number given day or block release only	11,164	8,012	6,330	5,540	3,801	2,481	2,333	2,009
Total trainees qualifying for grant	29,602	28,297	26,284	25,799	9,463	8,413	8,499	8,361
Total reported as completing first-year training (see note A)	35,512	30,632	27,687	26,564	10,284	8,846	8,750	8,547

NOTES:

A The total number reported included numbers not given day release and therefore not qualifying for grant from the Board. It is possible that numbers reported have been falling without a corresponding fall in the total numbers entering the industry, because employers are no longer reporting those who do not qualify for grant.

B The numbers reported as completing first-year training exclude many, but not all of those boys whose training terminated early.

[1] Ibid., Table 9, p. 53. Reproduced with the kind permission of the Engineering Industry Training Board through the Director Mr. Frank Metcalfe.

TABLE 8.3

Enrolments in National Certificate and Diploma Courses in Mechanical, Electrical and General Engineering 1968 and 1970

	O.N.C. and O.N.D.			H.N.C. and H.N.D.		
	1968	1970	Increase/ Decrease	1968	1970	Increase/ Decrease
Certificate registration						
Part-time day	18,754	15,347	− 18%	−	13,132	−
Block release	4,283	3,499	− 18%	−	610	−
Total part-time	23,037	18,846	− 18%	16,138	13,742	− 15%
Sat examination	15,261	11,924	− 22%	10,627	7,819	26%
Passed	9,452	7,190	− 24%	6,615	5,470	17%
Pass rate	62%	60%	−	62%	70%	−
Diploma registration	3,783	3,850	+ 1·8%	5,943	5,478	− 8%
Sat examination	1,637	1,660	+ 1·4%	1,997	2,530	+ 27%
Passed	1,107	1,187	+ 7·2%	1,638	1,998	+ 22%
Pass rate	68%	72%	−	82%	79%	−
Grand totals	26,820	22,696	− 15%	22,081	19,220	− 13%

Source: D.E.S., *Statistics of Education, 1970*, Vol. 3, *Further Education*.

TABLE 8.4

Pass rates (1965–70) in O.N.C. and O.N.D. Engineering examinations – final year

	1965	1966	1967	1968	1969	1970
O.N.C. students						
Enter	18,725	15,302	15,838	15,261	13,123	11,924
Pass	10,488	9,794	9,799	9,452	8,136	7,190
Pass rates	56%	64%	62%	62%	62%	60%
O.N.D. students						
Enter	1,191	1,081	1,319	1,637	1,557	1,660
Pass	784	786	903	1,107	1,032	1,187
Pass rates	66%	73%	68%	68%	66%	72%

Source: D.E.S., *Statistics of Education*, 1970, Vol. 3, *Further Education*.

The Committee on Technician Courses and Examinations. National Certificate schemes came into being in 1921 as a result in the first instance of consultations between the (then) Board of Education and the Institution of Mechanical Engineers. Other joint committees followed; representatives of the colleges as a third consultant group were added later. The aim was to make it possible for students to reach professional status through part-time study and in the early days industry and the colleges were allowed considerable flexibility in the planning and organisation of such courses. The scene changed: many more university students graduated in vocationally orientated subjects such as engineering and the institutions began to make it more and more difficult for the part-time student on the National Certificate route to achieve membership of a professional body. The H.N.C. is now being regarded primarily as a high grade technician qualification rather than a route to a profession and as its purpose changed the traditional curriculum began to be questioned.

The White Paper on 'Better Opportunities in Technical Education' (1961)[1] had initiated many changes but by 1967 it was already outdated by further developments such as, for example, the Industrial Training Act and C.N.A.A. degrees. The Secretary of State for Education and Science therefore invited the National Advisory Council 'to review the provision for courses suitable for technicians at all levels and to consider what changes are desirable in the present structure of Courses and Examinations'. Their report, in which the

---

[1] Cmnd. 1254, H.M.S.O.

above terms of reference appear on page 1, was published two years later.[1]

The technical education field was, and still is, the untidiest area of education and this was one of its greatest virtues. There were no fixed standards of entry, those who knocked on the door were admitted and courses were open-ended so that there was a choice of routes and a choice of exit points. The Haslegrave recommendations (they have not yet been implemented) are little more than a tidying-up and a tightening-up operation. The reasoning behind this runs somewhat as follows: the large number of joint consultative bodies administering the National Certificate schemes come to joint decisions slowly, if ever; the City and Guilds of London Institute, with a long history as an examining body for technical college students, is a large, efficient administrative empire and could well do the job better; training technicians should be a separate enterprise not just the first part of the training of technologists; the nomenclature of the technical college courses should mirror that of the jobs with which they are associated – craft courses for craftsmen, technician courses for technicians and so on.

The second paragraph of the report sets the scene. For the purposes of a proposed manpower survey the Committee on Manpower Resources for Science and Technology adopted a working description of the meaning of the term 'technician' which read:

> Technicians and other technical supporting staff occupy a position between that of the qualified scientist, engineer or technologist on the one hand, and the skilled foreman or craftsman or operative on the other; and that while there is an immense variety in the content of these occupations and the degree of expertise needed for them, the people who fill them can be broadly classified as 'technicians' for our purposes.[2]

The Haslegrave Committee adopted this definition for their quite different purposes since they knew 'of no single universally applicable definition of the term', nor did they attempt to devise one themselves since they felt 'that this would have been an exercise in trying to define the indefinable'.[3] To this inherent confusion must be added the fact that the proposed manpower survey was never actually completed because of the insuperable difficulties encountered in

[1] *Report of the Committee on Technician Courses and Examinations* (Chairman Dr. H. L. Haslegrave), H.M.S.O., 1969.
[2] Ibid., p. 3.   [3] Ibid., p. 3.

forecasting manpower requirements and the fact that the incumbents of industrial posts including the so-called technicians arrive by such a wide diversity of routes.

The conclusions and recommendations occupy six or seven pages of the report[1] and only the main proposals need be mentioned here. These are, first, the setting up of two new councils – a Technician Education Council (T.E.C.) and a Business Education Council (B.E.C.) responsible for planning, co-ordinating and administering technician and comparable courses, examinations and educational qualifications of a national character. The T.E.C. is to deal with technician courses and the B.E.C. is for courses in the field of business and office studies. 'An early task' for T.E.C. (and B.E.C. to some extent) would be to 'accept transfer' from the D.E.S. of the administrative work of the national certificates and diplomas and the City and Guilds of London Institute would then be invited to undertake the administrative work for both T.E.C. and B.E.C. The Committee foresaw that 'important practical issues would arise from this proposal' but felt they could be examined when the project was nearer realisation in principle. Three years after publication of the report there was no sign of a resolution of these issues.

The second main cluster of recommendations is concerned with the duration and types of courses and the nomenclature of the qualifications i.e. certificates or diplomas. In the case of the T.E.C. these would probably be named Technical (T.C. or T.D.) and Higher Technical (H.T.C. or H.T.D.). These are intended to be different from O.N.C./D. and H.N.C./D. and 'better suited to modern needs'. There would be 'better selection', a 'more feasible pattern of courses' and 'bridging studies' for some students at certain points. For the approval of such special arrangements 'sympathetic treatment' will be needed. It is 'hoped' that T.E.C. and B.E.C. will be 'actively encouraged' by the training boards who 'should' also 'give a sharp impetus' to the development of sandwich courses and more block-release courses with 'blocks of a length that would provide more time for study'. All the syllabuses 'should' prescribe general studies as an integral part of the course.

Towards the end of the recommendations the Committee concede that 'the completely voluntary approach to the grant of release *may be* insufficient' (my italics) to achieve the results considered to be essential and recommended that 'the Secretary of State for Education and Science should therefore consider in preparing the new Educa-

[1] Ibid., pp. 79–85.

tion Bill the possibility of including within it a measure to confer on every technician and comparable trainee a right to appropriate release to follow a course of further education associated with the training for his occupation.' How an employee would assert such rights against a reluctant employer is not discussed.

The changes envisaged in the Haslegrave report are administrative and semantic. A national certificate for technicians becomes a technicians' certificate administered nationally, not by a joint body but by City and Guilds personnel. If they do agree to take over the donkey work, they will in turn have to set up a series of 'bodies' of appropriate representatives to devise the syllabuses and the modules.

Once again 'better selection' is going to solve the failure problem, but we are given no hint of what selection procedures will do this. The cart has been constructed before we have provided a horse: given a society which wills the means and a government ready to set up a grants system for all types of student, forming committees to devise syllabuses and think up appropriate names for the awards could be done expeditiously with a minimum of fuss. Padding round the same ground 'hoping' for a miracle becomes a weariness and it is not surprising that it has taken so long to generate enough energy to start implementing the report. Rumour now has it that T.E.C. and B.E.C. are on the way, but it will need a more radical wind of change than that to impel the colleges on to an educational course appropriate for the twenty-first century.[1]

[1] The composition of the Technical Education Council was announced in March 1973. A chairman the B.E.C. was appointed in February 1974.

NOTE: The Industrial Training Act was amended in the Employment and Training Act of July 1973.

CHAPTER 9

Education for Living

While suggestions for tinkering with and patching up the examination procedures for part-time technical college students occasion almost total apathy, there is plenty of interest in the next Education Act and no shortage of 'priorities'. Everyone, indeed, has his own list and the needs of the sixteen- to eighteen-year-olds seem to appear on most of them.

In 1970 the Council for Educational Advance (C.E.A.) set out eleven targets for expansion. Many have a familiar ring echoing as they do proposals set out in the 1944 Education Act which are not yet implemented. The three of particular relevance to this chapter are numbers 7, 8 and 9 which read:

Increase opportunities for higher and further education;

Give youth a fair deal by providing every young worker with the kind of facilities provided for university students;

Set a date by which every young worker would have day release for further education and training.

Howard Glennerster, author of a subsequent pamphlet,[1] sets out the targets again[2] and discusses how we are to afford it. He argues that most industrial countries are planning to devote a rising share of their gross national product to education during the next decade and that the programme of the Federal German Government makes the C.E.A. proposals 'look modest by comparison'. He concludes: 'If education is to remain a social service because society believes this is necessary to ensure social unity and fair opportunities, this entails a larger public sector and rising taxes. The educational world must have the courage to say so. Society must will the means as well as the ends.'

Britain is now a member of the European Economic Community and the Treaty of Rome (Article 118) states that the Commission 'shall have as its task the promotion of close collaboration between

[1] *Willing the Means*, Council for Educational Advance, 1972. [2] Ibid., p. 16.

member states in the social field', and six particular items are listed concerning labour law and working conditions of which the third is 'basic and advanced vocational training'. The Council of the Community gave consideration to the 'General Principles for Implementing a Common Vocational Training Policy' in 1963 and in 1971 accepted and published a paper laying down 'General Guidelines for the Development of the Programme for Vocational Training at Community Level'.[1]

In the 1963 document there are ten Principles dealing with such matters as exchange visits, 'harmonising' the standards of examinations and the training of teachers. The second Principle sets down eight 'fundamental objectives' two of which are marginally related to the question of the *education* of the sixteen- to eighteen-year-olds as distinct from their vocational training.

Item c 'To broaden vocational training on the basis of a general education, to an extent sufficient to encourage the harmonious development of the personality and to meet requirements arising from technical progress, new methods of production and social and economic development';

Item d 'To enable everyone to acquire the technical knowledge and skill necessary to pursue an occupation and to reach the highest possible level of training, whilst encouraging, particularly as regards young people, intellectual and physical advancement, civic education and physical development'.[2]

One cannot perhaps expect anything more explicit than this from documents dealing with vocational training and for educational policy we must look to the Council for Cultural Co-operation. Member countries are already committed to a Decision of that Council taken in July 1967 to give priority to 'the implementation of the concept of lifelong education in the forward looking perspective of Europe 20 years ahead'.[3] The French Vocational Training Act came into force at the same time – July 1967 – and is in four parts embodying four laws. In presenting it the Prime Minister was joined by the Minister of Education and the Secretary of State for Education as well as the Minister of Labour – the first time that the Ministry of Education had been involved in laws governing vocational education. Part 4 of the Act states that 'lifelong vocational

---

[1] See *Vocational Training in the European Economic Community*, British Association for Commercial and Industrial Education, September, 1972.

[2] Ibid., p. 61.

[3] See *Continued Education* by E. W. Sudale, Council for Cultural Co-operation, Council of Europe, Strasbourg, 1971, p. 113.

training is a national obligation' and sees this as an integral part of lifelong education.

There are fears in some quarters that the European Commissioners will have too much power over the organisation of education in member countries.[1] Be that as it may, the writing on the wall is clear: the citizens of 1980, not only in Britain, but throughout Europe, will not be willing to tolerate restriction of educational opportunity. Those who wish to learn will demand the facilities to do so.

Early in 1968 the A.T.I. (Association of Technical Institutions), the A.P.T.I. (Association of Principals of Technical Institutions) and the A.T.T.I. (Association of Teachers in Technical Institutions) set up a joint working party to consider the education of the sixteen to nineteen age group. The title is, however, misleading. The twelve-page report[2] deals mainly with the overlap between schools and colleges in the provision of *full-time* education for this age group. It contributes nothing to the debate on the working of the Industrial Training Act and the need to *educate* as well as train young workers. Similarly Sir William Alexander (Secretary of the Association of Education Committees) in an address to the A.T.I.[3] discusses the problem of devising a new Education Act without mentioning educational provision for the army of young workers who have left full-time schooling at the earliest possible moment. In both documents it seems to be assumed that full-time education for everyone up to the age of eighteen is just round the corner.

The Labour Party in their pamphlet *Labour's Programme for Britain*[4] at least recognised the problem, but they were less than explicit about their plans and still 'hoping' that 'encouragement' will do the trick. Discussing the education of the sixteen- to eighteen-year-olds, they have this to say: 'Labour's objective is to offer *education for all* in this age group and our first priority will be to accommodate those to whom the education service at present offers nothing . . . Labour will . . . initiate discussion with a view to framing legislation designed to *encourage* continuing education. For example, it *should not be possible* to employ young people under 18, without making provision for their education and training.' (My italics.)

More recently the Labour Party has produced a paper on Higher

[1] See, for example, Lord Bowden's speech in the House of Lords, *Hansard* (Lords), 26 July 1972, cols. 1404–12.

[2] *16–19. An F.E. View*, A.T.T.I., London, April 1969.

[3] *Towards a New Education Act*, A.T.I., London, 1969.

[4] Transport House, 1972.

and Further Education[1] which is more explicit and contains a strong plea for a higher priority to be given to the 'tertiary' stage of sixteen to eighteen. Education beyond eighteen is subsumed logically enough under the title 'Adult Education'. All young people in the 'tertiary' stage should be considered as primarily in education and subsequently, if they wish, be day or block released for employment. Also recommended are mandatory grants for all over sixteen who are doing full- or part-time courses. No party in office would be likely to get away with such a Utopian document unconcerned with costs and other practical difficulties but – like the E.E.C. documents – it is on record and, whether quickly or slowly, such reforms will surely come.

Accepting then that the demand for education will go on growing; that the raising of the school leaving age to sixteen will be followed by an increase in the number of seventeen- and eighteen-year-olds continuing at school or college, the most important question is not how will it be organised or how will it be paid for, but what we, as adults, have to offer them. The A.T.T.I. is still 'hoping' that training under the Industrial Training Act can be combined with educational provision in the colleges and indeed in its recent submission to the Government has argued that initial training and education should be integrated under educational auspices.[2] However, the members of the Association do not speak with one voice on this subject which, in view of the diversity of provision in the further education sector, is hardly surprising. So far discussion of the possible educational content of such 'integrated' courses has understandably been vague and speculative since with no funds and no bodies there is little incentive to be more specific. Hugh Warren[3] is a protagonist of long standing in this cause and his views attract both admiration and criticism but there is little debate and almost no action.

It is time that the debate began if the staffs of colleges are to be prepared for the next generation of college students. There are of course some experiments: short courses for school leavers, vocational guidance conferences, industrial visits and so on; necessary and useful no doubt but insignificant in face of the need.

[1] Opposition Green Paper, *Higher and Further Education*, Labour Party, Transport House, London, S.W.1., January 1973.
[2] See Grinyer, Roger, 'Planning Council for All Further Education Urged', *The Times Higher Education Supplement*, 11.2.72.
[3] See his latest paper to the Association of Colleges for Further and Higher Education, *A Philosophy of Technical Education* and the subsequent discussion, A.C.F.H.E. Annual General Meeting, London, February 1972.

Because of the increase in student numbers in colleges and universities during the past ten years it is easy to underrate the size of the problem. This is analysed in Tables 9.1 to 9.4 which follow.

TABLE 9.1

School leavers 1967 and 1970 as a percentage of the relevant age-group population[1]

Age at 1 January	1967	1970
14	29·8	25·7
15	31·3	33·6
16	11·9	14·6
17	10·2	13·1
18 and over	5·7	6·7

In January 1970 the total of full-time pupils in schools of all kinds (in England and Wales) was 8·5 million of whom 3 million were in the 'secondary' sector. For many years now the number staying on beyond the statutory leaving age has been rising and as can be seen in Table 9.1 this general trend continued between 1967 and 1970. The actual number of leavers (from grant-aided and independent schools recognised as efficient) in the academic year 1969–70 was 614,210.[2] In the Fabian pamphlet *Planning for Education in 1980*[3] it is estimated that although the exponential trend must cease to hold 'at some fairly early point it could well be [that it] will in fact continue for five years longer'.

Table 9.2 presents the number in each age group over the school leaving age and the corresponding number who were *not* in attendance at school.

The next table (9.3) shows the destination of two year groups of leavers. In 1969–70 21·4 per cent of the school leavers continued in some form of full-time education leaving 78·6 per cent i.e. 482,600 persons – nearly half a million in a single year – *not* going on to full-time education.

We turn now in Table 9.4 to look at the numbers of young people up to the age of eighteen who are allowed day release from their employment. The discrepancy between the sexes is plain to see. The young women form roughly half of the work force in this age

[1] *Statistics of Education*, 1970, Vol. 2, *School Leavers C.S.E. and G.C.E.* Introduction, p. vii.
[2] ibid. Table 1, pp. 6–7.
[3] Fabian Research Series, No. 282, 1970, p. 17.

TABLE 9.2
**Young people over the school leaving age
not attending any school at 1 January 1970[1]**

Age at 1 January 1970	Numbers in age group	Numbers not attending schools (approx.)	% of age group (rounded)
15+ (over S.L.A.)	655,088	399,500	61
16	668,517	434,500	65
17	660,898	531,350	80
18	667,032	625,000	94
Sub-total	2,651,535	1,990,350	80[2]
19+	744,800	741,000	95·5
Grand total	3,396,335	2,731,350	85[2]

group and no more than 22 per cent of those granted day release. There are great differences between different types of industry. For example, Mechanical and Electrical Engineering industries release over 80 per cent of their young male employees and less than 30 per cent of the females. The distributive trades are the largest employers of young women and only 2 per cent of them had day release in 1970: the men fared little better and these trades are at the bottom of the pile with an overall release rate of 3·2 per cent. Heading the list are public administration and defence with a work force in this age range of approximately 20,000 equally divided between the sexes and a release rate of 90 per cent overall. Very few fifteen-year-olds are recruited (7 per cent in 1970) but anyone aged sixteen or seventeen joining H.M. Forces is pretty certain of opportunities for further education.

The final column in Table 9.4 indicates that now the leaving age has been raised to sixteen the colleges can expect a reduction of rather less than 13 per cent in the number of their day-release students, assuming the situation to remain static in all other respects.[3]

[1] Calculations based on Table 5, *Statistics of Education*, 1970, Vol. 1, *Schools*, pp. 10–15.
[2] Excluding fifteen-year-olds.
[3] This is of course unlikely. See Crampin, Alice, *Forecasting Student Numbers in Higher Education*, Higher Education Research Unit, London School of Economics, Reprint No. 37, 1969, in which the likely increase in school leavers with 'A' level qualifications is assessed.

TABLE 9.3

Leavers continuing in full-time education[1]

Destination	1966–67 (thousands)	1969–70 (thousands)	1969–70 Proportion of all leavers N = 614,000
Entering directly			
Universities	34·9	37·0	6%
Degree courses in F.E. establishments	4·7	5·5	<1%
Other courses in F.E. establishments	57·0	66·9	<11%
Colleges of education	19·4	20·0	3%
Total	116·0	129·4	21%
Temporary employment pending entry to further full-time education	3·6	2·7	0·4%

[1] Based on *Statistics of Education*, 1970, Vol. 2, *School Leavers C.S.E. and G.C.E.*, Introduction, p. ix.

TABLE 9.4

Proportions of students released by their employers during working hours for part-time day-release courses at grant-aided establishments[1]

England and Wales

	1966 Aged 15–17	1970 Aged 15–17	1970 Aged 16–17 only	Percentage reduction
Total insured	1,255,293	1,018,602		
Total released	265,278	243,945	213,197	
Percentage	21·1	24·0	—[2]	12·6
Males insured	615,086	490,889		
Percentage of total insured	49·0	48·2		
Males released	210,744	190,524	167,501	
Percentage of total released	79·4	78·1		
Percentage of males insured	34·3	38·8		12·1

[1] This table together with figures quoted in the related text is adapted from pp. 58–60 of *Statistics of Education*, 1970, Vol. 3, *Further Education*.

[2] Not recorded.

Instead of over a million young employees potentially available for part-time education, the number 'at risk' is likely to be of the order of 800,000. Any further reduction of this figure due to an increasing proportion electing to stay on at school beyond sixteen may well be offset by increasing numbers preferring to transfer to the colleges as full-time 'O' and 'A' level students. It is to be hoped that any space that is made available in the colleges will be used for experiments in non-vocational day release if the Government can be persuaded to pay for it. However, if the aim really is to provide educational opportunities for everyone up to the age of eighteen, something more than a few experiments which could only touch the fringe of the problem, will be needed.

Assuming that employers continue to offer day release to a quarter of their junior work force up to the age of eighteen, approximately 640,000 additional places would be needed for the remainder, about three-fifths of them for women: thus the work load in the colleges would be increased threefold. The estimated cost is £80 million i.e. £60 million more than at present.[1]

There is no sign that as a society we are prepared for this or convinced that there is any necessity for it.[2] The message from industry is that 'unqualified' school leavers are employable after a minimal initiation on the job. They may complain of the failure of the schools to educate them properly but they see no *economic* necessity to educate them further. The rest of us must surely ask what is the effect of this on the school leavers themselves and what would the educators do with them (and the use of the word 'with' is deliberate) if given the chance.

There are various ways of tackling this question. The number of young people opting for full-time education until eighteen – either at school or college – is increasing and is likely to continue to increase. The question of a suitable curriculum applies to them also and once we ask – what do they need to know? – we are immediately confronted with the question of the purpose of education.

Since in the U.S.A. schooling until eighteen is the norm it is natural to look to the other side of the Atlantic for some guidance.

---

[1] *Planning for Education in 1980*, ibid., p. 20.

[2] Professor Harry Armytage, in a typically breezy and stimulating paper addressed to the Association of Colleges for Further and Higher Education, was more optimistic and assumed that the colleges would rapidly become large Community Colleges on the American pattern and assumed further that his audience would be in agreement. *The Challenge to the Teacher*, A.C.F.H.E., 1971.

James Koerner has pre-empted the question with his essay 'A Candid Message to the English People'.[1] In the book of which the essay is a part the author deplores the view that only a relatively small proportion of children can benefit from a study of the basic academic subjects and is highly critical of the Newsom Report *Half Our Future*[2] which assumes, in his view, that at least half our children are unable 'to profit much from a secondary education centred on the fundamental subjects, which in fact, are the most vocational of all and which they may never study again if they fail to do so at school'. He warns us against following in the wake of 'yesteryear's educators in the United States' who also concluded that the majority of students being kept at school by law until sixteen and then to eighteen 'had neither the ability nor the desire to "profit from" (the usual phrase) the traditional academic curriculum. Obviously said our educators they needed something else. But what? Well, the reasoning went, they were interested in jobs, clothes, cars, movies and the opposite sex and so we should teach them something constructive about these things; and since they were all future citizens and founders of homes, they must be made interested, if possible, in "Citizenship" and "Home making". This blinkered view of the educational potential of the majority of children was shared alike, I regret to say, by great numbers of parents, teachers and educational administrators. The underlying assumption was a kind of modernised Platonism that divided children neatly by their I.Q.s and that many of your educators possibly deplore when it appears in other places in the educational system. The assumption turned out to be what in the current sociological jargon would be called "a self-fulfilling prophecy".'[3]

Koerner believes that 'education through the secondary level [which he assumes to be up to eighteen] should stress the basic academic subjects, the primary fields of human knowledge, and in doing so should stress the intellectual development rather than the vocational training or social adjustment of all children, bright, average and dull'[4] and his use of the word 'adjustment' should be noted. His trenchant criticisms of 'yesteryear's educators' in his country include additional warnings against a 'cafeteria' system with a wide choice of short courses in 'trivial' subjects (e.g. 'grooming' and 'dating') so that it is possible for a young person to go

---

[1] Koerner, James, *Reform in Education*, Weidenfeld and Nicolson, 1968, Chapter VIII, pp. 240–76.   [2] Central Advisory Council, H.M.S.O., 1963.
[3] Koerner, James, ibid., pp. 266–8.   [4] Ibid., p. 265.

through several years of schooling having learned nothing of sub-
stance in the basic subjects. These warnings spring from great dis-
illusionment with these early efforts at social education and they are
warnings which should undoubtedly be heeded but they do not deal
with the important question – which subjects of human knowledge
are the 'basic' or 'fundamental' ones and *how* should they be
'taught'? Our dilemma is implicit in Koerner's book but is never
made explicit. He adopts – surprisingly in view of his clear analytic
style in other contexts – either/or questioning to which in many
cases the answer could well be 'both'. Or he chooses emotive words
which indicate which alternative he sees as the 'good' one and which
the 'bad'. 'Education', he says, 'must be concerned with values' –
to which one can only add 'Amen' – and then goes on to ask 'Do
you want schools[1] to be places where children and young people
become literate in the basic subjects of human knowledge and *where
they try to equip themselves to live their personal and professional
lives as wisely as possible* . . . [my italics] or do you want (them) to
become an arm of the Welfare State, acting as child minding centres,
taking the place of, *by order of government* [my italics], inadequate
parents, ineffective churches and uncaring communities? Or do you
want them to become job-training centres taking the place of
industry and trades, which can do the training better?' We may opt
for his first alternative but we could not carry it out (the italicised
part of it in particular), without taking account of the social in-
adequacies delineated in the second. His objection to 'yesteryear's
educators' which I for one would share, is maybe, connected with
their apparently blinkered acceptance of existing society indicating
the norms of behaviour to which everyone should 'adjust'. In such a
context courses on 'homemaking' and 'citizenship' would indeed
merit the epithet 'trivial'.

On one level Koerner's is a traditional view of the educator's task
but in so far as he rejects 'trivial' domestication he has something in
common with the 'revolutionary' writers on education whose views
on the 'fear of freedom' and the education of the underprivileged
are far removed from conformist conditioning processes. For example
Paulo Freire writing about the title of his book *Pedagogy of the
Oppressed*[2] says that it is 'a pedagogy which must be forged *with* not
for the oppressed (be they individuals or whole peoples) in the
incessant struggle to regain their humanity'. Similarly Ivan Illich

[1] For 'schools' in Koerner's context read 'schools and colleges' in ours.
[2] Penguin Books, 1972. Translated by Myra Bergman Ramos.

calls upon his readers to escape from 'dehumanising systems' and to discover what must be done 'to use mankind's power to create the humanity, the dignity and the joyfulness of each one of us'.[1] These writers are writing from their experiences of the people of the Third World and mainly *for* them, but their works have implications for the first world ('oppressed' is a relative word) which many students of that world on both sides of the Atlantic are eager to endorse.

So: having used Koerner's advice in order to sort out some of the confusions which face us, we return to the question: given extra 'educational' time in the further education colleges, how should we use it? Clearly the 'second chance' aspect of these colleges must and will remain. Courses for 'O' and 'A' levels and other academic certificates will continue to grow for those who want them. Many of the others will be people who side-stepped school examinations and have chosen (or become obliged to take) jobs for which work-based training is all that is necessary. Most of them manage their lives reasonably well without benefit of educators. They see such people as irrelevant to their way of life because they see themselves as 'ordinary folk'. Statistically they are right – we are talking about the norm, the people with moderate intelligence, much practical 'nous', neither illiterates nor highflyers. In an educational system geared to educating the intellect, the danger is that large numbers of people will be made to feel inferior even to the extent of underrating what intellectual abilities they have. Avoiding this situation is not easy: it cannot be done by administrative procedures alone as studies of comprehensive schools have shown.[2] The class structure derives largely from the occupational structure and since occupation is related, however loosely, to ability and achievement which it is the business of the schools to encourage and promote, they are inevitably caught up in the 'social cleavages of class society'.[3]

In planning for this large average group one thing is quite clear: we might make a four-day week compulsory for the sixteen- to eighteen-year-old employees and compel them to attend a centre on the fifth day but we could *not* compel them to participate in any of our schemes. In the present social climate individuals insist on self-determination.[4] In their search for identity such young people

[1] *Celebration of Awareness*, Calder and Boyars, 1971.

[2] See Ford, Julienne, *Social Class and the Comprehensive School*, Routledge and Kegan Paul, 1969, pp. 138–42.

[3] Ibid., pp. 76–109.

[4] For an interesting historical résumé of recent changes in social structure and their educational correlates see Eggleston, S. John, *Towards an Education*

refuse to be told where to look – perhaps the most we can hope to do is to hold open a few doors and encourage exploration. This is a job for stalwarts and salesmen. So what have we, as educators, to sell? *Pace* Koerner, certainly not the kind of learning which involves desks and writing and examinations but something which, despite the warnings, I would call social education. This needs the teacher as a person and a robust, self-fulfilled person at that. The area of human experience which is basic to all young learners, whether brilliant, average or dull, is the area which is the most challenging to both teacher and learner: 'how to equip ourselves to live our personal and professional lives as wisely as possible', Koerner's own words in fact. This is not a subject which can be 'taught' in any didactic sense but it can certainly be discussed and explored in the company of an adult who is himself still an explorer. To quote Eggleston, 'If traditional status barriers are perpetuated in a situation where shared tasks are undertaken, conflict is a predictable outcome.' This is not to say that the teacher's experience counts for nothing – certainly not – but what is important is that in the shared learning situation 'the teacher must make his experience legitimate.'[1] Which, to spell it out, means 'logically admissible'. Attitudes to – say – religion, democracy, communism, capitalism, politics generally, sex, love, family life, social life, drugs, violence, crime – are picked up informally at home, at work and from newspapers, radio and television and we each build up our own conglomerate of prejudices in the process. All behaviour is learned and if we as adults do nothing to challenge ignorance and prejudice – whether in relation to dogmatically held religious beliefs, racial myths, class divisions, academic snobbery or any socially important topic – we have only ourselves to blame if more expert salesmen with other wares to sell win the day. If we want to promote tolerance, compassion, democratic attitudes, rational, responsible and informed behaviour then we must not leave it to chance. Social learning need not be dependent solely on family groups and peer groups of our own choosing, but can be promoted in mixed groups assembled for the purpose. We have learned a good deal about behaviour in groups, about the value of discussion for the clarification of ideas and the examination of points of view other than our own. The cathartic value of sharing anxieties either verbally by discussion or symbolically by means of

for the 21st Century: A National Perspective, Inaugural Address, University of Keele, 1970.

[1] Ibid., p. 37.

role-playing and drama is well recognised and we know how to train adults to do such work. What is needed is a commitment to its value and the worst mistake we can make is to imagine that emotional sensitivity can only be acquired by the highly intelligent.

Implicit in the foregoing is that the re-planning of the education of adolescents will require some re-education of adults. Educational provision cannot in fact be segmented: change attitudes in the primary schools and a pressure for change begins to be felt in the secondary schools. Parents, employers and teachers have to change if there is to be a radical change in the education of the adolescent. Change and education for change must go on throughout life. 'The making of an educative society will be necessary not only for children to reach their full potential as now estimated, but also to enlarge the pool of ability from which skill can be drawn. Here again the full development of the school system needs support from the education of the adults in the child's environment.'[1]

If the notion of permanent education – or recurrent education as I would prefer to call it – is to take root, then the use of all available facilities and resources – buildings and people – will have to be maximised. Schools and colleges will have to become multi-purpose educational institutions catering between them for all age groups in the community. Some local technical colleges have already dropped the restrictive adjective to become local colleges ready to respond to the general needs of the community as well as the specifically vocational ones. Naming is important and it is to be hoped that the trend will spread rapidly so that any individual, young or old, can identify the centre where his educational needs are likely to be met.

In addition to the adolescents such colleges should aim to attract two adult groups: those with skills and knowledge to impart and those seeking to acquire new skills and/or educational refreshment. Many individuals belong in both groups: there is no effective teacher who does not learn from his pupils and conversely few learners who do not have something to teach.

If local educators genuinely want a *college* as well as a training school the pious hopes must be abandoned and a plan of action devised. By the word 'college' I mean to imply a place where the *individual*'s educational and social needs are a prime concern. The local colleges are there – we have the bricks and mortar. They

---

[1] *Adult Education: A Plan for Development*, Report by a Committee of Inquiry (Chairman, Sir Lionel Russell, C.B.E.), H.M.S.O., 1973, para. 46.3 pp. 14–15.

155

could become lively centres of activity in the communities putting on all necessary courses for the academically inclined, encouraging all the liberal arts, providing down-to-earth teaching in practical crafts and a forum for free and responsible discussion of social and personal issues. The quality of the teachers would be crucial – the prime need is for reasonably cultivated people, on good terms with the younger generation, respecting their wishes and not over-anxious about their emotional problems – all this to be the first consideration. Each would then bring to the encounter his own expertise – be it in engineering or literature, music or current affairs – as a second string.

There is nothing doctrinal about such a programme – tolerance is of the essence and one cannot use force to indoctrinate tolerance. Nor is the pejorative use of the word 'permissive' appropriate. The reasoning behind the use of free and open discussion on controversial topics is widely misunderstood. Permitting people, even encouraging them, to express verbally what they genuinely feel cannot do harm: the parents and teachers who harm the young are those who don't *care* about how they feel. Indifference is the enemy, not freedom. We need not go all the way with the aphorism that nothing of any importance can be taught but there is no doubt that to *experience* justice, friendliness, concern, as a result of the behaviour of another person is more effective than a sermon.

Work of this kind is going on in small pockets all over the country, in schools, colleges and youth clubs, but it is unrecognised and dependent upon the enthusiasm of individuals who carry on despite the system. There are the inevitable 'administrative difficulties': 'L.E.A.s are interested in administrative neatness.' They prefer to know and have recorded 'who is where, when'.[1] In fairness one must add that enthusiasts can easily become monomaniacs and are often difficult colleagues: the important thing is not to lose sight of the priorities.

Nor must we forget that for the young *the* priority is the future. Alvin Toffler's best-selling *Future Shock*[2] must surely be required reading for all educators. In his chapter 'Education in the Future Tense', using the analogy of space flight, he makes the point that to avoid future shock as 'the total population of the technology-rich nations' speeds towards a rendezvous with super-industrialism (for

[1] See Trafford, Tony 'The End of an LEA Arts Centre', *Education and Training*, Vol. 13, No. 6, June 1971. Also Hunt, Albert, 'The Tyranny of Subjects' in *Education for Democracy*, Eds. Rubinstein and Stoneman, Penguin, 2nd edition, 1972, pp. 27–33.   [2] Pan Books, 1971.

which the book is a blue print) we must somehow manage to arrange 'a soft-landing'. 'Yet even as we speed closer, evidence mounts that one of our most critical sub-systems – education – is dangerously malfunctioning.'

'What passes for education today, even in our "best" schools and colleges is a hopeless anachronism. Parents look to education to fit their children for life in the future. Teachers warn that lack of education will cripple a child's chances in the world of tomorrow. Government ministries, churches, the mass media, all exhort young people to stay in school, insisting that now, as never before, one's future is almost wholly dependent upon education.

'Yet for all this rhetoric about the future, our schools face backwards towards a dying system, rather than forwards to the emerging new society. Their vast energies are applied to cranking out Industrial Men – people tooled for survival in a system that will be dead before they are.'[1]

In the rapidly changing philosophical climate in which such books are widely read and discussed, college students are increasingly unwilling to sit passively still and wait to be taught. *They* are likely to do some of the teaching and we must try to ensure that those in charge will be willing to listen. Probably one of the greatest immediate needs among this large body of young people is to learn to think well of themselves – not defensively out of a sense of inferiority but genuinely out of a sense of personal worth. In some, a healthy development of their own identity will have taken place under the benign influence of family and sensitive teachers but for those who have learned to despise themselves and hate the rest of us for allowing it to happen, the main hope is that they will encounter acceptance and respect before it is too late.[2] The most a group leader can hope to do on one day a week is to help them to find some topic or activity which excites them, gives them a sense of personal competence, and thus encourages them to rediscover their curiosity and go on learning. If we cannot offer them something which *they* see as an enrichment of their lives which helps them to face the future hopefully and constructively, we shall fail.

[1] Ibid., pp. 360–1.
[2] See Edgar Friedenberg's challenging study of American youth, *The Vanishing Adolescent*, written in 1959. Dell paperback.

APPENDIX I

Bibliography

Official Documents. H.M.S.O. Publications

WHITE PAPERS:
1961 *Better Opportunities in Technical Education*, Cmnd. 1254
1962 *Industrial Training: Government Proposals*, Cmnd. 1892

REPORTS:
Central Training Council
1967 *Second Report to the Minister*
1970 *Review of the Central Training Council*, Cmnd. 4335

Committee on Manpower Resources for Science and Technology
1966 *Report on the 1965 Triennial Manpower Survey of Engineers, Technologists, Scientists and Technical Supporting Staff*, Cmnd. 3102
1966 *Interim Report of the Working Group on Manpower Parameters for Scientific Growth*, Cmnd. 3103

Department of Education and Science. National Advisory Council on Education for Industry and Commerce
1969 *Report of the Committee on Technician Courses and Examinations* (Haslegrave)

Ministry of Education   Central Advisory Council
1959 *15 to 18* (Crowther)
1963 *Half our Future* (Newsom)

National Advisory Council on Education for Industry and Commerce
1966 Committee on Technical College Resources. *Report on the Size of Classes and Approval of Further Education Courses* (Pilkington)

Special Committee
1973 Committee of Inquiry. *Adult Education: A Plan for Development* (Russell)

CONSULTATIVE DOCUMENT:
Department of Employment
1972 *Training for the Future – A Plan for Discussion*

STATISTICS:
Department of Education and Science
1972 *Statistics of Education, 1970,* Volume 2, *School Leavers C.S.E. and G.C.E.*
1972 *Statistics of Education, 1970,* Volume 3, *Further Education*

Other Reports and Papers
1949 Scottish Council for Research in Education: *The Trend of Scottish Intelligence*
1969 Association of Teachers in Technical Institutions: *16–19. An F.E. View*
1969 Association of Technical Institutions: *Towards a New Education Act*
1970 Fabian Research Series 282: *Planning for Education in 1980*
1971 Council for Cultural Co-operation, Council of Europe, Strasbourg: *Continued Education* by E. W. Sudale
1972 British Association for Commercial and Industrial Education (B.A.C.I.E.): *Industrial Training – the Future Vocational Training in the European Economic Community*
1972 Council for Educational Advance: *Willing the Means* by Howard Glennerster
1972 The Labour Party: *Labour's Programme for Britain*
1973 The Labour Party: Green Paper, *Higher and Further Education*

Research Papers and Related Articles
Armytage, W. H. G. *The Challenge to the Teacher,* paper to Summer meeting, The Association of Colleges for Further and Higher Education, 1971
Bennis, Warren G. 'Leadership Theory and Administrative Behaviour', *Admin. Science Quarterly,* Vol. 4, 1959
Bowden, Lord. Speech in the House of Lords, *Hansard* (Lords), 26 July 1972, cols. 1404–12
Clark, Burton R. 'The "Cooling-Out" Function in Higher Education', *Amer. J. Sociol.,* Vol. LXV, No. 6, 1960
Cotgrove, Stephen. 'Education and Occupation', *Brit. J. Sociol.,* Vol. 13, No. 1, 1962

Crampin, Alice. *Forecasting Student Numbers in Higher Education*, Higher Education Research Unit, London School of Economics, Reprint No. 37, 1969

Eggleston, S. John. *Towards an Education for the 21st Century: A National Perspective*, Inaugural Address, University of Keele, 1970

Grinyer, Roger. 'Planning Council for All Further Education Urged', *The Times Higher Education Supplement*, No. 18, 11.2.72

Kahl, Joseph A. 'Educational and Occupational Aspirations of "Common Man" Boys', *Harvard Educ. Review*, Vol. XXIII, No. 3, Summer 1953

Morris, V. and Ziderman, A. 'The Economic Return on Investment in Higher Education in England and Wales', *Economic Trends* No. 211, May 1971

Pheysey, Diana C. Personal communication about the work of the Industrial Administration Research Unit, The University of Aston in Birmingham

Pugh, D. S. et al. 'A Conceptual Scheme for Organisational Analysis', *Admin. Science Quarterly*, Vol. 8, No. 3, 1963

Pym, Denis. 'Technical Change and the Misuse of Professional Manpower: Some Studies and Observations', *Occup. Psychol.*, Vol. 41, No. 1, 1967

Rudd, Ernest. 'Sample of Error', *The Times Educational Supplement*, 2.7.71, p. 4

Trafford, Tony. 'The End of an L.E.A. Arts Centre', *Education and Training*, Vol. 13, No. 6, June 1971

Vaizey, John. 'Ask a Silly Question', *The Times Educational Supplement*, 2.7.71, p. 4.

van der Eyken, Willem. Editorial, *Further Education*, Vol. 2, No. 4, Summer 1971

Venables, Ethel and Warburton, F. W. 'Relationship between the Intelligence of Technical College Students and Size of Family', *Eugenics Review*, Vol. 47, No. 4, January 1956

Venables, Ethel. *Placement Problems in Part-time Engineering Courses*, paper to Summer meeting, Association of Technical Institutions, June 1958

'One Subject Failures', *Technology*, April 1960

'Placement Problems among Engineering Apprentices in Part-Time Technical College Courses. Part I', *Brit. J. Educ. Psychol.*, Vol. XXX, No. 3, 1960

'Placement Problems among Engineering Apprentices in Part-Time Technical College Courses. Part II', *Brit. J. Educ. Psychol.*, Vol. XXXI, No. 1, 1961

'Changes in Intelligence Test Scores of Engineering Apprentices between the First and Third Years of Attendance at College', *Brit. J. Educ. Psychol.*, Vol. XXXI, No. 3, 1961

'Success in Technical College Courses According to Size of Firm', *Occup. Psychol.*, Vol. 39, 1965

'Educating England's Working Class', *College Board Review*, No. 57, Fall 1965

'The Human Costs of Part-Time Day Release', *Higher Education*, Vol. 1, No. 3, 1972

Warren, Hugh A. *A Philosophy of Technical Education*, Paper to the Annual General Meeting of The Association of Colleges for Further and Higher Education, London, February 1972

Books

Bennis, Warren G. *Changing Organizations*, McGraw-Hill, 1966

Bendix, Reinhard, *Work and Authority in Industry*, John Wiley & Sons Inc., New York, 1956

Blaug, M., Preston, M. H. and Ziderman, A. *The Utilisation of Educated Manpower in Industry*, Oliver and Boyd, 1967

Churchman, C. W. and Verhulst, M. (Eds.), *Management Sciences: Models and Techniques*, Vol. 2, Pergamon Press, Oxford, 1960

Douglas, J. W. B. et al. *All Our Future*, Peter Davies, 1968

Emery, F. E. and Trist, E. L. 'Socio-Technical Systems' in Churchman, C. W. and Verhulst, M. *Management Sciences: Models and Techniques*

Freire, Paulo. *Pedagogy of the Oppressed*, trans. Myra Bergman Ramos, Penguin Books, 1972

Friedenberg, Edgar. *The Vanishing Adolescent*, 2nd edn., Dell Publishing Co., New York, 1968

Ford, Julienne. *Social Class and the Comprehensive School*, Routledge and Kegan Paul, 1969

Glass, D. V. (Ed.) *Social Mobility in Britain*, Routledge and Kegan Paul, 1954

Goldthorpe, John H., Lockwood, David, Bechhofer, Frank and Platt, Jennifer. *The Affluent Worker*
Vol. 1 *Industrial Attitudes and Behaviour*, 1968
Vol. 2 *Political Attitudes and Behaviour*, 1968

Vol. 3 (*The Affluent Worker*) *in the Class Structure*, 1969 Cambridge University Press

Halsey, A. H., Floud, J. and Anderson, C. A. (Eds.) *Education, Economy and Society*, Free Press of Glencoe Inc., New York, 1961

Hunt, Albert. 'The Tyranny of Subjects' in Rubenstein, D. and Stoneman, C. (Eds.) *Education for Democracy*

Illich, Ivan. *Celebration of Awareness*, Calder and Boyars, 1971

Kahn, R. L., Wolfe, D., Quinn, R., Snock, J. D. and Rosenthal, R. *Organisational Stress: Studies in Role Conflict and Ambiguity*, John Wiley & Sons Inc., New York, 1964

Koerner, James D. *Reform in Education*, Weidenfeld and Nicolson, 1968

Layard, P. R. G., Sargan, J. D., Ager, M. E. and Jones, D. J. *Qualified Manpower and Economic Performance*, Allen Lane, London, 1971

Martin, F. W. 'An Enquiry into Parents' Preferences in Secondary Education' in Glass, D. V. (Ed.) *Social Mobility in Britain*

Percy, Lord Eustace. *Education at the Crossroads*, Evans Bros., 1930

Rice, A. K. *Productivity and Social Organisation*, Tavistock Publications, 1958

Rubinstein, David and Stoneman, Colin (Eds.) *Education for Democracy*, 2nd edn., Penguin, 1972

Toffler, Alvin. *Future Shock*, Pan Books, 1971

Turner, R. H. 'Sponsored and Contest Mobility and the School System' in Halsey, A. H., Floud, J. and Anderson, C. A. (Eds.) *Education, Economy and Society.*

Veblen, Thorstein. *The Theory of Business Enterprise*, Charles Scribner's Sons, New York, 1904

The Instinct for Workmanship, Norton & Co., New York, 1914

Venables, Ethel. *The Young Worker at College – A Study of a Local Tech.*, Faber and Faber, London, 1967

Wedderburn, Dorothy and Crompton, Rosemary. *Workers' Attitudes and Technology*, Cambridge University Press, 1972

Woodward, Joan. *Management and Technology*, Problems of Progress in Industry No. 3, H.M.S.O., London, 1958

Industrial Organisation: Theory and Practice, Oxford University Press, 1965

(Ed.) *Industrial Organisation: Behaviour and Control*, Oxford University Press, 1970

Skill Level from David Nelson's Classification of Occupations (1962)

1. Higher professional and administrative work

This group includes occupations which require university training to at least a three-year standard, and senior administrator occupations in commerce, industry, the Civil Service and local government. *Examples are:* Chartered Accountant, Actuary, Administrative Civil Servant, Advocate, Aeronautical Engineer (prof. qual.), Analytical Chemist, Architect, Attorney-at-Law, Bacteriologist, Barrister-at-Law, Biologist, Botanist, City Treasurer (when qual. Accountant), Civil Engineer (prof. qual.), Clergyman, Clerk in Holy Orders, Commissioned Officer in Regular Armed Forces, Company Secretary (if Solicitor), Dental Surgeon, Dentist, Director of Education, Economist, Electrical Engineer (prof. qual.), Entomologist, Geographer, Geologist, Graduate Teacher, Gynaecologist, Headmaster, University or College Lecturer, Mechanical Engineer (prof. qual.), Member of Parliament, Minister of Religion, Municipal Treasurer (when qual. Accountant), Naval Architect, Obstetrician, Oculist, Ophthalmic Surgeon, Pathologist, Physician, Physicist, Physiologist, Principal (Civil Service), Principal (College or University), Psychiatrist, Psychologist, Research Worker, Scientist (qual. scientific workers of all types), Solicitor, Statistician, Surgeon, Town Clerk (with degree), Under Secretary (Civil Service), University Professor, University Reader, Veterinary Surgeon.

Higher management with board status, men holding directive responsibility for an organistion, employers in more than a small way.

2. Lower professional technical and executive work

This group includes jobs which require several years of specialised training (and in most cases a background of advanced education), a variety of executive jobs of a more responsible kind and acumen.

Examples are: Chief Accountant, Advertising Executive, Agricultural Estate Manager, Architectural Draughtsman, Articled Solicitor, Artist, Assistant Master, Assistant Principal (Civil Service), Assistant Secretary (Civil Service), Author, Bank Manager, Bailiff, Buyer, Chief Constable, Company Secretary of Accountant standing, Critic, Director of small business, Dispenser, Engineering Draughtsman and Designer, Farmer (to include Cattle Farmer, Dairy Farmer, Horse Breeder, Stud Farmer, only if owner), Farm Manager, Film Producer, Forestry Officer, Journalist, Manager of medium-sized factory or business house or of major branch of big organisation, Departmental Manager, Manufacturer, Hospital Matron (qual.), Librarian (Fellow), Optician, Parliamentary Agent, Pharmacist, Physiotherapist, Planning Engineer, Probation Officer, Schoolmaster, Scientific Technician, State Registered Midwife, State Registered Nurse, Surveyor, Teacher, Transport Manager (50-plus employees).

3. Highly skilled workers

This group includes highly skilled craftsmen with special training and a fair amount of responsibility, some of the more responsible and exacting commercial jobs and most industrial supervisory jobs. *Examples are:* Assistant Accountant, Air Hostess, Commercial Artist, Carpet Planner (measuring, making up and laying carpets), Stockbroker's Cashier, Clerk of Works, Accountants Clerk, Senior Accounts Clerk, Bank Clerk with responsibility (4-plus under him), Legal Clerk, Solicitor's Clerk, Commercial Traveller, Draughtsman, Estate Agent, Electrical Fitter, Machine Shop Foreman, Manager of small store (outfitters), Masseuse (female) with qualifications, Senior Monitor, Certificated Nurse, Air Pilot, Senior Retail Salesman in large establishment, Private Secretary, Shorthand Typist with qualifications, Laboratory Technician, Teller, Toolmaker.

4. Skilled workers

This group includes trained skilled workers (technical, clerical) and some personal services. *Examples are:* Boiler Maker, Cabinet Maker, Canvasser, Carpenter, Cashier, Accounts Clerk, Booking Clerk, General Clerk, 'middle range' Clerk, Coach Builder, Dressmaker with training, Engine Driver, Heating and Ventilating Engineer, Fitter, Furrier, Ladies' Hairdresser, Lithographer, Machinist, Monitor, Children's Nurse (qual.), N.C.O., Pattern Maker, Policeman, Printer, Shop Assistant, Professional Sportsman, Station Master, Senior Storeman, Tailor,

Turner, Routine Typist with qualifications, Upholsterer, Warrant Officer, Wood Machinist.

5. Moderately skilled workers

This group includes certain of the less technical tradesmen such as: Bricklayers, House Painters, Plasterers, Plumbers, Sheet Metal Workers, Welders.

A wide range of the more skilled factory operatives in the metal, chemical, textile, etc. industries.

A wide range of store and transport workers such as: Despatch Clerk, Bus and Tram Driver, Railway Guard, Railway Signalman.

A wide range of workers in certain of the personal services such as: Barber, Butcher (hand), Boot Repairer, Filing Clerk, low-grade Clerk, Tally Clerk, Cook and Housekeeper, Dressmaker (poor grade), Dressmaker's Cutter, Fireman, Gamekeeper, Goods Checker, Horse Groom, Lorrydriver, Tailor's Machinist, Miner, Child Nurse (unqualified), Panel Beater, Private in Regular Armed Forces, Proprietor of small boarding house, Quarrying Operative, Receptionist, Junior or Ordinary Shop Assistant, Storeman, Taxi Driver, Telegraphist, Telephone Operator, Telephonist, Threshing-Machine Worker, Typist (unqualified), Head or Senior Waiter.

6. Semi-skilled workers

This group includes many factory operatives engaged on semi-automatic machines, assembly etc., and domestic transport and personal service workers of the sort: Caretaker, Chambermaid, Cinema Usherette, Bus and Tram Conductor, Window Cleaner, Dairy Hand, Deliveryman, better graded Domestic Servant, Truck Driver, Hospital Orderly, Routine Machinist (single items only), Lady's Maid, Milkman, Mother's Help, Park Keeper, Parlourmaid, Porter, Postman, Scaffolder, Ticket Collector, Waiter, Waitress, Woodman.

7. Unskilled workers

This group includes persons engaged in unskilled labour or coarse manual work, and includes: Automatic-Machine Operator, Chimney Sweep, Bus Cleaner, Office Cleaner, Contractor's Labourers and Navvies, Daily Help, Dock Labourer, lower grades of Domestic Servants, Dustman, Labeller, Labourers, Laundry Hand (folder, junior), Kitchen Maid, Packer, Presser (automatic), Road Sweeper, Stoker.

APPENDIX III

Additional Tables

TABLE A3.8

Opportunities for finding a job

In relation to schooling

Sample	Schools	Ratings							
		Very satisfactory and satisfactory		Fair		Poor and very poor		Totals	
		N	%	N	%	N	%	N	%
O.N.C. respondents	Selective	103	57·5	50	28·0	26	14·5	179	100·0
	Modern	95	43·4	75	34·2	49	22·4	219	100·0
	Other	8	42·1	9	47·4	2	10·5	19	100·0
	Totals	206	49·4	134	32·1	77	18·5	417	100·0
O.N.C. interviewees	Selective	29	61·7	10	21·3	8	17·0	47	100·0
	Modern	23	39·6	22	38·0	13	22·4	58	100·0
	Other	2	33·3	4	66·7	0	0	6	100·0
	Totals	54	48·7	36	32·4	21	18·9	111	100·0
Trade respondents	Selective	13	61·9	3	14·3	5	23·8	21	100·0
	Modern	90	58·1	42	27·1	23	14·8	155	100·0
	Other	4	50·0	4	50·0	0	0	8	100.0
	Totals	107	58·2	49	26·6	28	15·2	184	100·0
Trade interviewees	Selective	6	85·7	0	0	1	14·3	7	100·0
	Modern	23	57·5	12	30·0	5	12·5	40	100·0
	Other	2	100·0	0	0	0	0	2	100·0
	Totals	31	63·3	12	24·5	6	12·2	49	100·0

Opportunities for finding a job

In relation to level of father's job   *Row percentages*

		Ratings							
		Very satisfactory and satisfactory		Fair		Poor and very poor		Totals	
Sample	Level of father's job	N	%	N	%	N	%	N	%
O.N.C. respondents	Professional	30	50.0	23	38.3	7	11.7	60	100.0
	Skilled	144	49.7	92	31.7	54	18.6	290	100.0
	Semi- and unskilled	21	51.2	11	26.8	9	22.0	41	100.0
	Totals	195	49.9	126	32.2	70	17.9	391	100.0
O.N.C. interviewees	Professional	8	53.3	6	40.0	1	6.7	15	100.0
	Skilled	39	50.6	24	31.2	14	18.2	77	100.0
	Semi- and unskilled	3	30.0	3	30.0	4	40.0	10	100.0
	Totals	50	49.0	33	32.0	19	19.0	102	100.0
Trade respondents	Professional	11	91.7	0	0	1	8.3	12	100.0
	Skilled	70	56.0	33	26.4	22	17.6	125	100.0
	Semi- and unskilled	15	48.4	14	45.2	2	6.4	31	100.0
	Totals	96	57.1	47	28.0	25	14.9	168	100.0
Trade interviewees	Professional	2	100.0	0	0	0	0	2	100.0
	Skilled	25	75.8	5	15.1	3	9.1	33	100.0
	Semi- and unskilled	3	30.0	6	60.0	1	10.0	10	100.0
	Totals	30	66.7	11	24.4	4	8.9	45	100.0

TABLE A4.2

Distribution of respondents according to type of first employment as apprentices

| | Respondents | | | | | | Interview sample | |
| | 1950–52 samples Manchester | | 1957–60 samples Birmingham | | All respondents | | | |
Type of employing firm	N	%	N	%	N	%	N	%
Manufacturing industry according to type of product:								
a) Simple articles with few or no components e.g. metal castings, screws, gears	24	11	45	11	69	11	15	9
b) Small articles with many components e.g. small pumps, domestic gadgets, instruments	26	12	80	19	106	17	28	17
c) Large articles, many components e.g. heavy machinery, motor cars	95	43	160	38	255	40	72	44
d) Others	13	6	22	5	35	5	7	4
1. Total in manufacturing firms	158	72	307	73	465	73	122	74
2. Contracting firms	36	>16	65	>15	101	>15	22	>13
3. Public bodies e.g. local authorities, post office	24	11	47	11	71	11	20	12
4. Others e.g. newspapers	1	<1	2	<1	3	<1	1	<1
Grand totals	219	100	421	100	640 (NK = 4)	100	165 (NK = 1)	100

NK = not known.

TABLE A4.10
Job changes

Number and type of changes	All respondents				Interview sample				
	Before 21		After 21		Before 21		After 21		
	N	%	N	%	N	%	N	%	
1. None	409	63·5	31	4·8	87	52·4	21	12·7	1.
2. One, two, three or more, same firm	50	7·8	288	44·7	19	11·5	50	30·3	2.
3. One different firm	49	7·6	88	13·7	14	8·4	22	13·3	3.
4. Two different firms	72	11·2	100	15·5	25	15·1	27	16·4	4.
5. Three or more different firms	57	8·8	103	16·0	18	10·8	39	23·6	5.
6. Left engineering	7	1·1	34	5·3	3	1·8	6	3·7	6.
Totals	644	100·0	644	100·0	166	100·0	165	100·0	
							(1 NK)		

NK = Not known.

TABLE A4.14

Size of firm and type of instructor

(1957 O.N.C. cohort)

Column percentages

$N = 228 = 97\%$ of 236

Type of instructor	Size of firm by number of employees		Totals	N
	I, II & III 999 and below	IV 1000+		
Mainly by full-time instructor	15	50	36	**83**
Supervisor	17	10	13	**29**
Olderworker or no-one in particular	68	40	51	**116**
Totals	100	100	100	
N	**90**	**138**		**228**

Chi squared between extreme ratings $\dfrac{14 \mid 69}{61 \mid 55} = 26 \cdot 28$

$p < 0 \cdot 001$

TABLE A4.15

Size of firm by place of training

(1957 O.N.C. cohort)

Place of training	Size of firm by number of employees			Totals	
	I & II 249 and below	III 250–999	IV 1000+		
	Col. %	Col. %	Col. %	Col. %	N
(i) Works training school	14	19	43	33	75
Row %	8	12	80		100
(ii) At the bench	53	31	26	32	73
Row %	30	21	49		100
(iii) Throughout works	14	17	20	18	41
Row %	15	19	66		100
(iv) Drawing office	14	15	3	8	17
Row %	35	41	24		100
(v) Site and field work	0	12	>4	5	12
Row %	0	50	50		100
(vi) No special training	5	6	<4	4	10
Row %	20	30	50		100
Totals	100	100	100	100	
Row %	18	21	61		100
N	42	48	138		228
					(8 NK)

The sample used in this table is the 1957 cohort – O.N.C. only – the largest and most homogeneous sample available. Percentages can be compared with those given for the total respondent sample in Tables 4.1 and 4.5, pp. 50 and 53. Size of firm was not available for all respondents.

65 per cent of respondents checked one or other of the first two categories for place of training. Proportions rose as size of firm increased for those trained in works training schools and fell for those trained at the bench.

	I, II, III	IV
(i)	15	60
(ii)	37	36

Chi sq. = 14·3   p <0.0005

TABLE A4.16
Size of firm by type

Randomised (interview) sample
1957/1960 only
Column and row percentages

| *Type* | *Size of firm by number of employees* | | | | | |
	I 99 and below Col. %	II 100–249 Col. %	III 250–999 Col. %	IV 1000+ Col. %	Totals Col. %	N
(a) Simple articles Few components	0	7	7	>8	7	**7**
Row %	0	14	14	72		100
(b) Small articles Many components	> 29	36	33	>8	19	**20**
Row %	25	25	25	25		100
(c) Large articles Many components	> 29	14	27	60	44	**47**
Row %	11	4	8	77		100
(d) Others	0	14	0	>3	4	**4**
Row %	0	50	0	50		100

Total manufacturing	59	71	67	80	74	**78**
Row %	13	13	13	61	100	
Contractors	41	29	33	2	16	17
Row %	41	24	29	6	100	
Public Bodies	0	0	0	18	10	**11**
Row %	0	0	0	100	100	
Grand total	100	100	100	100	100	
Row %	16	13	14	57	100	
N	**17**	**14**	**15**	**60**		**106**

Over half of the respondents had trained with firms with more than 1,000 employees, and the other three sizes were equally represented among the rest. Among firms making small articles with many components (Type (b)) e.g. domestic gadgets, pumps, all four sizes were equally represented. Types (a) and (c) (small castings and heavy machinery) and Public Bodies were predominantly large. Very few contractors employed more than 1,000 people and 41 per cent employed less than 100. Percentages can be compared with those in Tables 4.1 and 4.2, pp. 50 and 51.

Table A4.17
Size of firm by scale of production (Manufacturing only)

Scale of Production	Size of firm by number of employees								Randomised (interview) sample 1957/1960 only Column and row percentages	
	I 99 and below Col. %	II 100–249 Col. %	III 250–999 Col. %	IV 1000+ Col. %	Totals Col. %	N
1. Small batch One-offs/Prototypes	89	30	> 33	28	36	**27**
Row %	30	11	11	48	100	
2. Large batch	11	30	> 22	17	19	**14**
Row %	7	22	14	57	100	
3. Mass production	0	0	> 33	49	35	**26**
Row %	0	0	11	89	100	
4. Continuous flow	0	10	0	6	5	**4**
Row %	0	25	0	75	100	
5. Other	0	30	> 11	0	5	**4**
Row %	0	75	25	0	100	
Totals	100	100	100	100	100	
Row %	12	13	12	63		100
N	9	10	9	47		75

The first three categories for scale of production account for 90 per cent of the respondents from manufacturing industry (cf. Tables 4.1 and 4.3, pp. 50 and 52). Most of the very small firms represented were engaged on one-offs; firms of all sizes engaged in large

Table A5.1

Reasons for change of course and/or college

Sample	Total N	No changes or no answer		Total answering question		Reasons for changes					
		N	% of Total N	N	%	Course not available at first college *or* new college more convenient		New course more appropriate		Course easier	
						N	%	N	%	N	%
1950 respondents	78	56	72	22	100	14	63·6	8	36·4	0	—
1952 respondents	144	118	83	26	100	17	65·4	9	34·6	0	—
1957 respondents	236	111	47	125	100	77	61·6	30	24·0	18	14·4
1960 respondents	188	115	60	73	100	54	74·0	16	21·9	3	4·1
All respondents	646	398	61	246	100	162	65·8	63	25·6	21	8·6
O.N.C. respondents	443	243	55	200	100	129	64·5	52	26·0	19	9·5
Interviewees	166	97	58	69	100	38	55·0	26	37·7	5	7·3

TABLE A6.1

Job level and technical college achievement after the age of twenty-one

Maximum examination success by 1966

Job level	O.N.C. interviewees N = 115 = 69% of total										Trade interviewees N = 51 = 31% of total									
	O.N.C. total		1. Less than 2		2. O.N.C. final (C.&G Year 5)		3. H.N.C. Year 1		4. H.N.C. final and beyond		Trade total		1. Less than 2		2. C.&G. Year 5 (O.N.C. final)		3. H.N.C. Year 1		4. H.N.C. final and beyond	
	N	Col %	N	Col %	N	Col %	N	Col %	N	Col %	N	Col %	N	Col %	N	Col %	N	Col %	N	Col %
2. Lower Professional	**40**	35	**8**	15	7	17	4	29	**21**	70	**8**	16	4	10	1	13	0	0	3	11
Row %	100		20		17		10		53		100		56		11		0		33	

3. Highly Skilled	**48**	**24**	**13**	**3**	**8**	**19**	**14**	**5**	**0**	**0**
	42	44	54	43	27	37	35	62	0	0
Row %	100	50	27	6	17	100	75	25	0	0
4. Skilled	**23**	**19**	**3**	**0**	**1**	**18**	**16**	**2**	**0**	**0**
	20	35	13	0	3	35	40	25	0	0
Row %	100	83	13	0	4	100	89	11	0	0
5/6. Moderately and Semi-skilled	**4**	**3**	**1**	**0**	**0**	**6**	**6**	**0**	**0**	**0**
	3	6	4	0	0	12	15	0	0	0
Row %	100	75	25	0	0	100	100	0	0	0
Totals	**115**	**54**	**24**	**7**	**30**	**51**	**40**	**8**	**0**	**3**
	100	100	100	100	100	100	100	100	0	100
Row %	100	47	21	6	26	100	78	16	0	6

TABLE A7.6

Question: If you have, now or in the future, a son of your own, would you say whether and in what way, you would like his educational opportunities to differ from your own

Type of comment	Total respondents		Total interviewees		O.N.C. respondents		O.N.C. interviewees	
	Total N	Total %	Total N	Total %	Total N	Total %	Total N	Total %
I Longer education and more full-time								
(i) Selective schooling and/or university	130	30	47	32	102	34	35	34
(ii) Longer full-time education. Obtain best certificate possible. One day a week a poor substitute	76	17	23	15	47	15	14	14
(iii) Sandwich courses and/or block release. Earning while you train very attractive. Good employers and proper educational provision	53	12	25	17	36	12	19	19
Sub-total I	259	59	95	64	185	61	68	67
II Present system with improvements								
(iv) Vocational education at school. More realistic practical training and development of aptitudes. More helpful and understanding	83	19	20	14	53	18	13	13
(v) Would depend on him and his abilities	25	16	8	5	19	6	4	4
(vi) No differences	72	6	25	17	46	15	16	16
Sub-total II	180	41	53	36	118	39	33	33
Total I + II	439	100	148	100	303	100	101	100

	439/644	68	148/166	89	303/443	68	101/115	88
III End selective schooling								
(vii) Comprehensive education	30	5	7	4	25	6	6	5
(viii) Less streaming and specialisation – more liberal (arts) education at school and college	40	6	11	7	30	7	8	7
(ix) Dissatisfied with present system of entry to grammar schools	17	3	0	0	13	3	0	0
Sub-total III	**87**	**14**	**18**	**11**	**69**	**16**	**14**	**12**
Total answering question	**526**	**82**	**166**	**100**	**372**	**84**	**115**	**100**
IV No answer	118	18	0	0	71	16	0	0
Grand total	**644**	**100**	**166**	**100**	**443**	**100**	**115**	**100**

APPENDIX IV

Questionnaire

PRESENT ADULT OCCUPATION

AND TECHNICAL COLLEGE ACHIEVEMENT

DURING APPRENTICESHIP

A FOLLOW-UP STUDY

NUFFIELD RESEARCH UNIT,
DEPARTMENT OF EDUCATION,
UNIVERSITY OF BIRMINGHAM,
BIRMINGHAM, 15.

STRICTLY CONFIDENTIAL

INITIAL COLLEGE ....

INITIAL COURSE ....

NAME ....

ADDRESS ....

....

1	2	3

4	5	6	7

I. BIOGRAPHICAL DETAILS

	Day	Month	Year
Date of birth:			

8	9

Age on leaving school:................................

Type of school attended:

Grammar	
Technical	
Secondary Modern	
Comprehensive	
Other	

10	11	12

How many older brothers have you? .... How many younger? ....

How many older sisters have you? .... How many younger? ....

Father's job (please be as specific as possible) ....

13	14

List here any certificates obtained at school (e.g., U.E.I., 'O' levels, etc.). Give details.

Certificate	*Subjects Passed*
....	....
....	....
....	....
....	....
....	....
....	....

15	16	17

1

II. INDUSTRIAL EXPERIENCE AND TRAINING

What is the title of your present position? ....

18	19

How many persons, if any, do you directly control? ....

Do you work in: a drawing office?   ..   ..   ..

or a workshop? ..   ..

Put a tick in appropriate box

or a laboratory? ..   ..

or (specify)? ....

20	21	22

How many persons work in the same room? ....

Our record shows that during your first year at ....

Technical College you were employed by ....

[ ] *Tick here if this is accurate.*

If not, correct here ....

23

List here the jobs you have held since leaving school.   Give an exact description with dates:
Up to 21:

JOB	FIRM	DATE
....	....	....
....	....	....
....	....	....
....	....	....

24	25
.	

After 21:

JOB	FIRM	DATE
....	....	....
....	....	....
....	....	....

If you held an apprenticeship or learnership between the ages of 16 and 21, what was it called? (e.g., apprentice draughtsman, technical or trade apprentice, etc.)

....

26	27

Did you sign indentures? ....

2

Where did you receive your works training?

In the Works Training School .. .. ..

In part of workshop set aside for training .. ..

At the bench .. ..

Elsewhere (specify) ....

28

Comment: ....

....

By whom was it given?

Full time instructor .. ..

Supervisor .. ..

Older worker .. ..

Other person (specify) ....

No one in particular .. ..

29

Comment: ....

....

How long did it last?

More than a year .. ..

Up to One year .. ..

Up to Six months .. ..

A few weeks only .. ..

30

Comment: ....

....

What did you think of the works training you received?

Very good .. ..

Fairly good .. ..

Moderate .. ..

Rather poor .. ..

Unsatisfactory .. ..

31	32

Comment: ....

....

3

The answers to the next two questions should relate to the firm in which you did most, if not all, of your technical training and which allowed you to attend technical college.

Type of Firm:

Firms can be divided roughly into the following three types:

(*a*) Manufacturing .. .. ..

(*b*) Contractors .. ..

(*c*) Public bodies .. ..

Indicate with a tick to which of these your firm belonged.

Complexity of Product:

For those who put a tick by 'Manufacturing' in the previous question.

(1) What type of product did your firm make?

(*a*) Simple articles with few or no components, e.g., metal castings, screws, gears .. ..

(*b*) Small articles with many components, e.g., small pumps, domestic gadgets, instruments .. ..

(*c*) Large articles with many components, e.g., heavy machinery, motor cars .. ..

(2) What was the scale of production?

(*a*) "One off" and small batches, e.g., prototype equipment, special orders .. ..

(*b*) Large batch production, no assembly line, e.g., car bodies, castings, plastic goods .. ..

(*c*) Mass production, assembly line processes, e.g., household articles, electric motors, motor cars .. ..

(*d*) Continuous flow, e.g., manufacture of paint, chemicals, plastic

If none of the above seem appropriate, describe the product here:

....

....

....

4

III. TECHNICAL COLLEGE EDUCATION

BETWEEN THE AGES OF 16 AND 21.

The records we have of your examination results are listed below. Please tick if correct, enter any necessary alterations on the dotted line, and complete.

Year.	Course taken.	Exam. result. i.e., Pass, Fail, Absent.	College.	Tick here
19___				☐
Correction				
19___				☐
Correction				
19___				☐
Correction				
19___				☐
Correction				
19___				☐
Correction				

36	37	38	39

40	41	42	43

44	45	46	47	48

Where there has been a change of college and/or course, give reasons.

....

....

....

49

Can you now look back and comment on your college career. For example, do you have any regrets?

....

....

....

50

If further education was continued after the age of 21, list details below.

....

....

....

51	52

5

If you obtained some certificate as a result of your college studies, complete Section III(a). If not, turn to Section III(b).

Section III(a). *For those successful in some technical college examinations.*

Were your studies recognised in any way by your firm, e.g., bonus, increase in wages, promotion? Please give details and comments.

....

....

....

....

53	54

Is it a condition of your present appointment that you must have attained a particular technical qualification? If so, state which. Add comments.

....

....

....

....

55

Do you consider the technical certificate you now hold is:

Essential .. .. ☐
Desirable .. .. ☐
Of some value .. .. .. ☐
Irrelevant .. .. .. ☐

for your present position?

56

How far have you used the knowledge you gained at college in your industrial job?

(i) Mathematics .. ..

Regularly	
Occasionally	
Very rarely	
Never	

(ii) Science .. ..

Regularly	
Occasionally	
Very rarely	
Never	

57

6

·(iii)   Workshop Practice .. .. ..

Regularly	
Occasionally	
Very rarely	
Never	

(iv)   Other subject (specify):

....

Regularly	
Occasionally.	
Very rarely	
Never .. ,. ..	

58

(v)   Other subject (specify):

....

Regularly	
Occasionally	
Very rarely	
Never	

mment: ....
....

oking back, do you think the years of study were worth while:

For the job you do .. ..

Yes, definitely .. .;	
Yes, on the whole ..	
Uncertain	
No, on the whole ..	
Definitely not	

59

For personal satisfaction .. ..

Yes, definitely	
Yes, on the whole ..	
Uncertain	
No, on the whole ..	
Definitely not	

yes to either question, in what way? ....
....
....

60	61	62

7

If not, why not? ....

....

....

If uncertain—discuss: ....

....

....

III(b) *For those who left college without obtaining a certificate.*

Did you attend college throughout the five years of your apprenticeship?

Yes	
No	

For those answering Yes:

Though you failed to obtain a qualification, do you feel your studies were of some value to you? If so, in what way. If not, why not? Add comments.

....

....

....

For those answering No:

Was the decision to give up your technical college studies before reaching the age of 21 made (*a*) by you, or (*b*) by your employer?

(*a*) If your own decision, what were your reasons?

....

....

....

....

(*b*) If the firm's decision, what were their reasons?

....

....

....

....

....

....

....

king back on the years from leaving school to becoming an adult worker, would you
that the opportunities you had for finding a job to your liking were:

Very satisfactory	
Satisfactory	
Fair	
Poor	
Very poor	

atisfied, say why:

....

....

....

....

ot, what improvements would you like to see for your own sons?

....

....

....

....

ou have, now or in the future, a son of your own, would you say whether, and in what
, you would like his educational opportunities to differ from your own?

....

....

....

....

9   (P.T.O.

V.

We hope to arrange interviews with about one in ten of the respondents to this questionnaire.

If you are willing to talk to an interviewer for about half an hour, please state here where you could meet (e.g., home address or work) and what time of day would be convenient.

Please do not write in this column

Place of interview	
Possible times	

72	73	74

75	76	77

78	79

Index

197